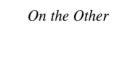

On the Other

On the Other
A Muslim View

RUSMIR MAHMUTĆEHAJIĆ

Translated by Desmond Maurer

FORDHAM UNIVERSITY PRESS
NEW YORK 2011

Previously published as *Malo znanje: O drugome u muslimanskim
vidicima* (Zagreb: Antibarbarus, 2005).

Fordham University Press has no responsibility for the persistence
or accuracy of URLs for external or third-party Internet websites
referred to in this publication and does not guarantee that any
content on such websites is, or will remain, accurate or
appropriate.

Fordham University Press also publishes its books in a variety of
electronic formats. Some content that appears in print may not be
available in electronic books.

Library of Congress Cataloging-in-Publication Data

Mahmutcehajic, Rusmir, 1948–
    [Malo znanja. English]
    On the other : a Muslim view / Rusmir Mahmutćehajić ;
translated by Desmond Maurer.
        p.   cm.— (Abrahamic dialogues)
    Includes bibliographical references.
    ISBN 978-0-8232-3111-9 (cloth : alk. paper)
    1. Religious tolerance—Islam.   2. Violence—Religious
aspects—Islam.   3. Islam—Relations—Christianity.   I. Maurer,
Desmond.   II. Title.
    BP171.5.M3613   2011
    297.2′8—dc22

                                                    2009049678

Printed in the United States of America
13 12 11   5 4 3 2 1
First edition

In the name of God, the All-Merciful, the Ever-Merciful!

Contents

Preface   ix

1.   I, Thou, and He   1
2.   The One and the Many   7
3.   The Stranger   13
4.   Self-Knowledge   20
5.   The Sense-of-Self and the Debt   27
6.   Being-at-Peace   34
7.   Faith   41
8.   Beauty   47
9.   The Hour   53
10.   Humanity   59
11.   The Other and the Different   66
12.   Intolerance I   73
13.   Intolerance II   80
14.   The Muslim   87
15.   The Universality of Prophecy   94
16.   The Nation of the Just   101
17.   Dialogue   107

18. Finding Fault with Others and the Self 114
19. Free Will and the Covenant   120

Afterword: The Text and Its Power   127
Notes   135
Bibliography   161
Conceptual Glossary   165

Preface

This essay is essentially about a question, the question of tolerance as viewed from the point-of-view of a muslim.[1] It may be that posing the question within clearly defined limits and giving a decisive explanatory role to those limits will produce an answer. What is certain is that an unclear question will produce an unclear answer, which in turn will render unclear the limit separating question from answer, the pre- from the post-liminal, "is" from "is not."

Both question and answer are addressed to potential readers, the intended recipients of this account, most of whom the author, naturally, does not know. The text mediates between individual readers and the author. The author, generally speaking, cannot know by what, how, when, or where his unknown readers' *sense-of-self*[2] has been formed. He cannot know their gender, age, or race any more than he can know why or how they will approach the text. All he can be sure of is that they must know the language it is written in. To experience the text as a relationship with its author implies a common language. They may be reading it in another language, but then a translator will have intervened, and the mediate experience will be a weave of author with text, translator, translation, and reader. What stubbornly endures between author and reader, however, is the essence that inheres in linguistic form and is transferable from one language to another, accessible to every human consciousness, no matter that the translator's mediation remains a tertium quid, never fully known to either reader or author.

Whether through the original or translated text, then, the reader will join the author in addressing the question of tolerance. Both author and reader must admit that each of them knows his or her self better than they do anyone else. They must also admit that this knowledge is never total. Compared to Him,[3] Who has full knowledge, both author and reader are, in their different ways, ignorant.

For the questioning to take shape, certain key terms—*tolerance, being, muslim, point-of-view*—must be explored in a sufficient variety of contexts to make clear the concepts' semantic ranges. In this way, we will also determine for each concept its contrary—*intolerance, non-being, non-muslim, absence of view*.

In doing so, this discourse could proceed to its uncertain reception without addressing a matter of crucial importance for it: namely, the question of author and reader: who they are, who it is who discourses, and who it is who reads. Everything expressed here is expressed by *someone*, of whom it is a trace, but the very meaning of the question of author and reader has paled and faded as a result of our turn toward the external world and our preoccupation with its images, which, as human experience expands, seem increasingly fatal. Alas, an individual may come to know the external world and act in it, even though his inner world remain in shadow, unknown. Under such circumstances, the question of who gathers and who relates knowledge comes to seem less important than the knowledge itself or the simple act of relation.

Traditional wisdom holds that the knowing subject can be accessed only through his or her[4] knowledge, and that being and knowing are inseparable: Being entails knowing and, conversely, knowing entails being. This contrasts with modern science, which admonishes us to concentrate on what is said rather than on who says it, as it considers the object of knowledge independent of the knowing subject. This second approach neglects being and ignores the knowing subject almost entirely, for knowing *does* belong to being and, conversely, being to knowing. The distinction between them cannot be reworked so as to produce two fully distinct particulars. Similarly, this text cannot be divorced from its author or the infinite dialectic of being and knowing. The author, as an individual, has consciousness and a point-of-view. They are part of what makes him human. Everything he says unfolds from within that point-of-view. That is the only way something can be said. It does not matter that some elements of his discourse may have been taken over from others, through listening to them speak or reading their works. In one way or another, they have become part of the being of the discoursing subject. They are there because of countless connections with others. Present in the author's self, they form a stable relationship with what was already there, developing relations of connection and separation, exclusion and inclusion. Whatever the author's being has received, it can give. Giving is what has made it capable of receiving. It is the same with questioning and answering, albeit each occasion is different. Nor are any of the author's points-of-view fixed inalterably. They change from moment to moment, and both question and answer are constantly changing images.

The questioning subject is a human being. This entails a changing point-of-view. In this irresistible flux, the subject finds itself posited in relation to self, body, family, community, people generally, earth and heaven, and everything in between. It cannot confine itself to any one of these levels of being, the boundaries of which are subject to change and to recognition. Being oneself precludes denial of the encompassing chain that stretches from the lowest depths of human being to the furthest heights of the external world. We are travelers and seekers. The key question for each of us is: Where are we traveling and what are we seeking?

Confessing one's belonging to any of these levels of being means, in the end, affirming that one belongs to them all. Wherever one happens to be, it is one's destination and one's goal that determine the relationship between being and knowing. And that relationship is

never immutably fixed. Every moment brings a new position to replace the old.

Tolerance, which may be glossed as suffering, putting up with, or
enduring, is a way of relating to the boundaries of the self. It involves
recognition of the boundaries between different levels of being, where
human being begins and ends, without ever completing either the
process of beginning or that of ending. In this relationship, the self
may exalt itself above or humiliate itself before the other. Both involve assessment and valuation. But, "tolerance" is a word in language and so is used in an infinity of expressions. Every human
moment is unique, as are all human expressions and acts of interpretation. Depending on the expression, the meaning of tolerance changes.
In textual discourse, too, the meaning of the term "tolerance" changes
from context to context. We have to do with its meaning both within
and beyond certain limits with regard to a certain religious identification and the concepts associated with it, in the hope that we may discover elements that speak to each and every reader while respecting
his or her human uniqueness.

Point-of-view may be designated in a variety of ways, but never so
as to entirely exclude or encompass the individual's situatedness in an
environment, from the very core of self (and even deeper) up to and
beyond the furthest star. Identity may be designated muslim, christian,
or jewish, but first and foremost, it is human. No other form of identity
overrides the human identity. This identity situates the individual in the
totality of existence—with everyone now alive but also all those who
came before or will come after. Being-with-oneself entails being-with-
everyone, and that entails boundaries, albeit constantly changing ones.

Each individual's (sense of) self is formed separately and differently from every other. No two selves can ever be equated. As a result,
this study on tolerance does not assume that the word means exactly
the same thing to any two readers. The irreducible difference of every-
thing-that-is allows change to take place in two directions—toward
the Principle or away from It. That each individual self is unique does
not abrogate the meaningfulness of dialogue. The opposite is true, in
fact. It is only through dialogue that involves an infinite number of

points-of-view that both directions can be known and the one that leads to the Principle can be chosen, albeit with full freedom to abandon it at any moment. That is why any such dialogue explores the full range of meaning from sense to its denial. The value of any given dialogue will naturally vary, depending on point-of-view.

The relationship between writer and reader corresponds to that between master and student. The first gives, the second receives. For this to be possible, the first must once have been in the same position as the reader is now. All mastery is attained through long and uninterrupted study. This brings the student into contact with many teachers, at different times and in different parts of the world. Receiving from them has inducted the student into a chain of tradition that passes from master to student, always preserving the intimate relationship of being and knowing. Everything received through such tradition faces the supreme test of being realized in the recipient. This endless chain of receiving and giving may be called muslim, christian, or jewish. Its substance will be tested over time in all the individuals who belong to it or adhere to one of the denominations. Each tradition is a journey and a quest. The names may be borne by all sorts of people, but the goal of the journey is not refuted by their distance from it.

When we consider a/the muslim point-of-view, it is always as the position of an individual. This point-of-view has been shaped, however, by the greater or lesser influence of those who have received it and passed it on, at different times, in different places, languages, and societies. It may be validated by personal self-realization or by evidence of the historical experiences of others, but it is also validated by the fact of being expressible in any language. When dealing with a single term that has been used at various times and places to designate a point-of-view, one should be at pains to determine what its adherents agree on, or at least on what a majority agrees. The following questions therefore become crucial: Which points-of-view may be termed muslim? Where is the source of these points-of-view, and what is their goal?

These are questions for each and every individual. They come to expression in each of us and they exist across the whole range of being, from humanity's inner core up to and beyond the final limit of existence. Only by situating the concept of the muslim point-of-view within a sufficient number of contexts will we be able to confirm its range from the lowest levels of existence to the Principle and also understand how it may contribute to the self-realization of each member of that part of humanity properly denominated muslim.

The term *muslim* is to be found today in all languages. Its history may be traced back from those languages to its use in the *Qur'an* or Recitation, where it witnesses to the Prophet's transmission of that which God revealed to him. The context of its appearance in the Book will make clear its meanings and how they have been received by the inheritors of that tradition, as well as the potential for distortion and forgetting. This context may then be compared with how those meanings have transferred into other languages. That relationship is subject to variation, to which both the unchanging text, expressed as it is in terms of human aims, and the changeable individual, with all the situations through which he or she may pass, contribute. The relationship is one of changing interpretation. Moreover, no individual can attain self-realization without changing the interpretation of everything that makes up his or her being and knowing.

There is one more thing of importance to note for the reader. For any understanding of human beings and the world(s) as a whole, whereby the harmony of the two and the return to God may be realized, it is important to accept that there are two types of knowledge: namely, one which resides in the heart of human being, independent of any form of external authority, and a second that is taken over or received from outside and must always depend on some form of external authority. According to the traditional view of the world, the second form of knowledge is only a reminiscence or recollection of the first. The first form of knowledge is decisive for our self-realization as human beings, while the second may be of use to self-realization but also counterproductive for it. The distinction between these two forms of knowledge is foundational to the entire discourse, but proper discussion of this subject would have required lengthy digression. For the sake of coherent exposition, we have decided not to include it in this book. Any reader curious to know more of this distinction will have to look for it elsewhere.

NOTE ON THE TRANSLATION

Shortly after publication in Bosnian, this book was translated independently into English twice. The first translation was made by Shahab Yar Khan, the second by Desmond Maurer. The author has decided to use the Maurer translation. Both translations attempt to deal with complex issues of how to reconnect key discursive terms of the islamic intellectual tradition with their original semantic chains, connection to which is almost invariably obscured by semantic petrification or ideological distortion. This has not been a simple or entirely successful undertaking, but it is to be hoped that it may contribute to the explanation of obscurities and the passionate response they evoke in contemporary heirs to the tradition of the Prophet Muhammad as well as illuminating for other observers how this tradition is interpreted and practiced by both individuals and societies.

The author wants to express his gratitude to both translators, as well as to the many readers who have publicly expressed their views on the book.

And if thy Lord had willed, whoever
is in the earth would have believed,
all of them, all together. Wouldst Thou
then constrain the people, until
they are believers?

They will question thee concerning
the Spirit. Say, "The Spirit is of
the bidding of my Lord. You have
been given of knowledge nothing
except a little."

Qur'an, 10:99 and 17:85

1. I, Thou, and He

Tolerance is a relationship between one human being and another or others.[1] We tolerate the other or others, who are, as a result, tolerated. This is an inevitable aspect of human being, which is finite being (that is, both with and within limits). These relationships are established either on the same levels or among different levels. The tolerating subject may be humble or arrogant vis-à-vis the tolerated. The reasons for taking one attitude or the other are crucially important for both parties. Any discussion of the relationship of tolerance from a muslim point-of-view must begin by noting that the word *muslim* signifies primarily a relationship between an individual and God and subsequently that individual's relationships with other people or the world. The relationship with God determines our mode of being and without knowledge of it no further conclusions may be drawn regarding any other relationship.

Each of us experiences a constant desire for self-realization in Peace.[2] Self-realization is keeping the self on the path toward the Real. Only the Real is total Peace. Peace is both the source and goal of human being. In Arabic, Peace is *al-Salām*, one of the names of God. An individual who desires God as *al-Salām* is *muslim*. The relationship of the *muslim* to God as *al-Salām* is peacefulness, being-at-peace, or *islam*.[3] This mode of being is common to everything in existence. We participate in or exclude ourselves from it by our own free will, which is, however, limited or finite. Beyond those limits, we are subject to Peace, and our relations with Him are therefore both voluntary and necessary. We are in essence both being and knowing. Our journey and quest include the return to Peace, as realization of all the possibilities of being-and-knowing. For something to be comprehended in our being-and-knowing, it must be brought into connection with the Real. Whenever being-and-knowing are separated from the Real, the terms *muslim*, *islam*, and *al-Salām* cease to apply. Such separation is a part of human life, so that the quest for the being and the meaning of these ideas is the substance of humanity at its best.[4]

When in *islam* (at peace), we derive from it our approach to ourselves, others, and the world as a whole. Through this mode of being, we bear witness to the whole. Our relationship to the whole is relationship to God as first cause and final destination. To say "I" is to recognize being within boundaries determined by the Thou of all existents and by their infinity. Recognition of being admits its inseparability from knowing. The I-Thou pair is always an expression of Him as Unity or the One. Given that no pair can comprehend or negate that Unity, every Thou is a partial revelation of Him. Total knowledge, which would encompass everything, can be attained neither in nor without the other. This is why suffering or tolerating the Thou is a precondition of the dignity of the self and involves recognition of Him, regardless of difference.[5]

Although the One is in everything, He may be approached only through His revelation in the many, just as time, which exists through countless infinite moments, may be approached only through that flow.

To discuss tolerance from the muslim point-of-view, one must first understand how the sense-of-self of the freely self-professed muslim is shaped. Even though naming is a precondition of revelation and so of coming to know that which is, knowing a name is not the same as knowing what it names. We are constantly relating to ourselves at all levels of the self, as well as to phenomena around us, in all their diversity, and to the world as a whole. Relating to a given thing entails sacrificing a prior relation. To relate is to live. But living also means recognizing death and finding an answer to questions regarding death. This may all be understood as an expression of the One to Whom everything belongs and nothing can be added. The One, Who reveals Himself in countless manifestations without ever becoming one of them, requires of us that we make our peace with Him and take rest from all multiplicity and movement. This goal is with, in, and beyond the world. Human being is both remembrance and forgetting. We realize ourselves only through remembrance, though without ever escaping the threat of forgetting.

No attainment can be final, and we are expected not to prejudge irreducible difference out of our limited ignorance. We are asked, by the mere fact of existence in determinate form, to tolerate, bear, or suffer that difference with regard to both possibilities—both that which is superior and that which is inferior. Nor is that all. The simple fact of being created relates or connects us to everything that is. Human being is I with regard to every other individual Thou and with regard to them all together. The sense-of-self gets lost in alterity, when intimacy excludes the One.

Viewed from a muslim point of view, the self is related to everything through the One. That does not, however, fix the self, as the One is at once absolutely proximate and absolutely remote. This is the mode of *being-in-the-moment* that involves breaking the connection with phenomena external to the One so that the self may relate to them through Him. The individual's relationships with the self, the world, and the One are consequently in constant flux.

Tolerance is the relationship between an individual who tolerates and something tolerated. It is the acceptance, sufferance, and bearing of something different than what the one accepting, suffering, or bearing either is or will be. The tolerated may be an individual, a group, or a thing. And there is no individual who does not tolerate, as no sense-of-self can exist without a social and natural environment. Every sense-of-self, both individually and collectively, is formed by language, signs, and interpretations. Its particularity extends to the boundaries of other linguistic, symbolic, or semantic systems. Neither contact with nor relation to these other systems is inalterable. These systems are, in fact, constantly changing, as is the sense-of-self. Language, signs, and semantic references, inseparable from relations with the other and the different, perdure within an interpretative community, whose members inherit and come to possess them through connecting them internally and differentiating them from other communities. Each person's sense-of-self is determined by this connection with the other. Others are its boundaries, and, consequently, sense-of-self is always also that other. "I am" is only possible insofar as it coexists with "I am not." Excluding the other also means excluding the sense-of-self itself, which is simultaneously "I am" and "I am not."

Interpreting tolerance means, principally, interpreting the sense-of-self of the tolerating subject. But this sense-of-self is not unchanging. Every sense-of-self is composed of unique attributes—spiritual, bodily, and social. They are reflected in will, faith (love and knowledge), and virtue. They are affected by everything an individual comes into contact with. The sense-of-self itself changes as the subject's understanding of what it is related to changes. Other individuals, groups, and things are also subject to change. They are always different from the individual in contact with them. This difference is shaped by the tolerating subject's sense-of-self and may be entirely opposed to the contents that determine it. As a result, tolerance covers a wide range, from the very near to the very far, from the very similar to the very different.

Given that there is always a quantifiable greater or lesser distance between the subject and any other or Thou it comes in contact with, and given that the subject necessarily knows that other less well than its own self, any prejudice in their immediate relationship will always be to the detriment of the other or Thou. That cost cannot be removed by reducing the relationship to one of agent and patient. Only by confessing that the knowledge of both is necessarily incomplete can their relationship approach justice through the One.

Tolerance is therefore an important aspect of every individual's dignity. How it is understood and applied determines how harmonious a subject's relationship with himself, others, and the world as a whole will be. Only by accepting the inevitability and meaning of Thouhood or otherness can one come to see journeying and seeking, from which the sense-of-self cannot be separated, as purposeful. Such a way of looking allows the meaning and rights of everything in existence to be affirmed so that they are seen in relation to the whole, from the void to the Absolute, and also seen, like everything else, to be returning to the Absolute.

When the tolerating subject is muslim, the relationship to others includes jews and christians, as well as followers of other traditions. It also includes Muslims, who are indifferent to how the tolerating subject is formed and who deny or set up against it the entirely different formation of their own selves. When the tolerating subject is muslim, his task is to answer questions as to how and why individuals and groups whose individual or group identities have been formed differently (within the jewish, christian, buddhist, or hindu, or other traditions) should be tolerated. The same question can be asked from the perspective of each of these other forms of group affiliation, as well as to those within the boundaries of each community who are hypocrites with regard to major aspects of the self or who oppose the principles of their tradition, and so forth.[6]

Dealing with these questions from the muslim point-of-view means bringing together important aspects of the muslim sense-of-self, on the one hand, and aspects of the tolerated self, on the other. The crucial question regarding the relationship between the muslim and others is the question of the muslim himself. For us to know why we do or do not tolerate something or someone, we must first know who we are ourselves. Such knowledge cannot be final or closed. Every determination of the self as muslim entails recognition that it neither is nor can be the one and only closed form. Given that we can know God through knowledge of ourselves, coming to know the other and the different is conditioned by self-knowledge. But God is fundamentally and irredeemably other and different. No knowing can comprehend Him, but He comprehends everything in His own knowing.

Whatever answer we give regarding tolerance and intolerance of the other and difference, to be valid from the muslim point-of-view, it must be justifiable in terms of journeying and seeking—finding God and realizing sublimity of character as the only goals. Presentation of the whys and wherefores of muslim tolerance of the jewish or christian other will be aided by a look at the most important aspects in the formation of the muslim sense-of-self. In our discussion, we will focus on these whys and wherefores.

One cannot consider, determine, or interpret the principal reasons for muslim tolerance of the other and the different, or the limits of that tolerance, without first addressing the question, "What is the most important factor in shaping the muslim sense-of-self?" Learning about and presenting the muslim sense-of-self is a matter for interpretative communities. Those communities are both many and various. The relations between interpretative communities determine how far opinion and behavior may swing from one degree of tolerance to another. Given that every interpretative community is conditioned by historical and social circumstances, its presentation of the other and the different is shaped by the ways its collective sense-of-self has been formed.

Amongst Bosnian Muslims, the most common traditional oaths are sworn by one's *din*, which is to say, by one's debt to God.[7] Examples include the phrases *Dina mi*, *Tako mi dina*, and *Moga mi dina,* all of which mean some variant of "By my *din*." This concept of *din* appears to be a major determinant of the muslim sense-of-self. For one who swears by his *din*, there would appear to be no more important determinant of the deepest content of the self. That is the reason behind the popular muslim saying: "Surrender your head, if you must, but your *din*, never!" What, then, is *din*? What in its development provides grounds for tolerating, for example, christians and jews? These issues touch the character of humanity, which is open to development from any given stage toward a better one. The ideal is to attain perfect character, which is to say a good and beautiful one. Attaining this, we realize our highest potential.

2. THE ONE AND THE MANY

Looking at how an individual relates to self or an environment made up of both similar and different people, we can distinguish certain behavior as clearly unacceptable and undermining of that individual's or of other people's dignity. If that person is a declared Jew, Christian, or Muslim, the unacceptability of his or her attitude toward others and the different may be examined from the point-of-view he or she claims to belong to and not just those they consider alien. Insofar as Jewish, Christian, or Muslim individuals all consider their affiliation total, unacceptable behavior can be interpreted as representing a degree of underrealization of the self within those traditions. No human life is exempt from the probability of such deficient realization.

Not infrequently, this causes us to question the traditions themselves rather than their self-declared adherents. If one wants to see what possibilities a tradition in fact offers, then one should assess the unacceptable views, opinions, and behavior of individuals in terms of the best models tradition has to offer. Nor do the traditions just offer ideal models. There are clear examples of the formation and realization of such models in goodness and beauty. History is filled with examples of evil and ugliness. They may, however, be counterbalanced by the presentation of evidence of goodness and beauty.

What makes a particular model or ideal jewish, christian, or muslim, in any real sense? What is it founded on and how may it be followed? These questions require elucidation before labeling unacceptable phenomena harmful to human dignity "Jewish," "Christian," or "Muslim." If judaism, christianity, and islam are paths toward God, which He has revealed—which jews, christians, and muslims confess them to be—then the phenomena of evil and ugliness are issues of deficient self-realization and do not refute the traditions in their authentic meaning.

According to the divine discourse given through the Prophet as the Recitation, associating anything with God is unforgivable sin (idolatry).[1] He is One, and there is no god besides Him. This is the most evident content of human consciousness. Intolerance of any and all idolatry is needed to grasp creation as manifold and as the relationship of all that participates in it.

> God forgives not that aught should be with Him associated; less than that He forgives to whomsoever He will. Whoso associates with God anything, has indeed forged a mighty sin.[2]

Witness to divine Unity is the beginning and end of the Recitation. That is the essence of the discourse of all of God's prophets, from Adam, the first human being and first prophet, to Muhammad, the perfect example of the human act of praising God and the seal of His prophets.

Only God is unlike anything, and only He cannot be compared with anything. No condition of the human will is severable from consciousness. When consciousness is informed by witness to Unity, it shapes the will. It makes us intolerant of the denial or covering over of Unity. But both are human possibilities, like remembrance and forgetting. If these possibilities did not exist, there would be no free will, nor any confidence (good faith) between God and humankind as mutually faithful, insofar as God makes and we receive the offer of a relationship based on good faith. Free will, which grounds the relationship, allows us this choice, because we are creatures. This simply means that we are in existence and so in a world of binary oppositions or pairs. Creation entails that in and alongside everything there appears a counterpart or pair: "And everything created We two kinds; haply you will remember."[3]

These pairs are an ever-present manifestation or evidence of Unity. They are always linked to each other, directly or through the Unity they reveal. These links are a bond that is constantly coming-into-being and fading before the One. The One is both infinitely remote and infinitely near to everything. It is in the nature of everything to be a sign of the One. As such, each sign is connected to every other one, just as each sign is itself an internally differentiated pair through which the One manifests Himself and bears witness of Himself. We are called to realize ourselves in the One and with Him, through the appeal to and remembrance of God, who is One. The human capacity to call on God testifies that He is near. But, as He cannot be limited, His nearness is absolute:

And when My servant questions thee concerning Me—I am near to answer the call of the caller, when he calls to Me.[4]

So remember Me, and I will remember you.[5]

We indeed created man; and We know what his self whispers within him, and We are nearer to him than the jugular vein.[6]

Just as His nearness is absolute, God is also infinitely remote and cannot be compared to anything finite: "And equal to Him is not any one!"[7] and "Like Him there is naught!"[8]

Given that He reveals Himself in His creation through His names, those names divide between absolute closeness and similarity, on the one hand, and absolute remoteness and incomparability, on the other. Thus, there are the names of Beauty, Gentleness, and Mercy as well as those of Majesty, Severity, and Wrath. So, too, every phenomenon in the world has its pair. In this difference, Unity is revealed. Being in such a world and with it, all pairs reveal divine Unity to humanity. Although these pairs ensure ceaseless motion, their principle is Peace. From Him they come, and to Him they return.

We may consider a thing sufficient in itself and separate it from its "other side," converting it from a signifying sign into a self-contained existent confined to itself or the world. This possibility is due to our free will. But in doing so, we deny the divine Unity as expressed in the confession: "I testify that there is no god but God." As a result, in one of a practically infinite number of ways, whether a thing, an idea, or a human impulse, something from His creation comes to be associated with God. This is violence by ourselves against ourselves. Through it, our openness to infinity is closed off. We are reduced and confined to the quantifiable world. None of these forms of violence can overcome the constant flux of relations in the binary world and its revelation of the One. Nor can we remain entirely cut off from the general presence of the divine names. Human will is not absolute. Human freedom is conditioned or finite.[9] Final judgment is subject to God's mercy, which is all-encompassing and surpasses even His wrath.[10]

> Say, "O my people who have been prodigal against yourselves, do not despair of God's mercy; surely God forgives sins altogether; surely He is the All-forgiving, the All-merciful.
>
> "Turn unto your Lord and find peace in Him, ere the chastisement comes upon you, then you will not be helped. And follow the fairest of what has been sent down to you from your Lord, ere the chastisement comes upon you suddenly while you are unaware."[11]

In the case of different peoples—with different languages, different ways of serving God, other races, and so forth—they are themselves signs in the general diversity of creation that speak of the one true God. Everyone, every individual, is original and authentic, as is the dignity in each of them. The whole of humanity inheres in each individual, and vice versa. Everything that belongs to difference is revelation of Unity: "God created you and what you make."[12] Doing justice means recognizing that Truth abides with everything in the world and that, accordingly, everything is a sign of Truth. When that is denied or covered over in the things of the world, they are spoilt or, to put it differently, we commit injustice against the signs around us and so against ourselves.

Given that, as creatures in the world, our nature is binary, our judgment always depends on comparison or measurement. So does our knowledge. But, not even the totality of the levels of existence exhausts Unity. Consequently, in whatever we do God remains other, an inevitable and insurmountable difference, so that all our knowledge is conditioned. This difference is for God to announce,[13] and He alone, as the One Whose knowledge comprehends all, can judge entirely justly and without distinction, as nothing is other to Him or to His knowledge. Justice is the presentation of the Truth. And complete presentation is the Truth itself.

Every phenomenon in existence, as a distinct manifestation of Unity, is created. That is why the Truth of the Creator is with the creatures. It can never pass into human understanding without remainder or difference. Therefore, recognition of difference or otherness in every person and every sign in heaven and on earth and everything between is inseparable from recognition and witness of God. No human judgment can overcome the difference that exists between things. All things, as created, are at peace in Unity, from whence they came into existence and to which they will return. Difference is from God and with Him. Our debt to it is also a debt to God, Who is the first and final judge: "And follow Thou what is revealed to thee; and be Thou patient until God shall judge; and He is the best of judges."[14]

We cannot realize our desire for being-at-peace unless our goal is absolute Peace. Being-at-peace is the relationship of the peaceful one to God as Peace. This is the meaning of the Master's discourse of the person-of-peace (*muslim*), being-at-peace (*islam*), and Peace (*al-Salām*).

We are in the created world, and we are creatures ourselves. Both human being and the world span a range from the void or extreme dispersion to Unity and Peace. The purpose of our being is to find Unity and Peace in everything. This is the finding of God or the return to Him. Thus we open ourselves toward Peace, to return to Him. Our opening toward Peace and journeying toward Him is distilled as a lesson in The Opening,[15] which the people-of-peace repeat during the standing part of prayers: "Guide us in the upright path, the path of those whom Thou hast blessed."

This prayer to God, uttered by the individual, that He guide people onto the right path, refers to the horizontal axis of human existence, from which we can ascend or fall but on which we may also wander unable to reach the final goal. Ascension is the finding of God in everything in both the inner and the outer worlds and recognizing each thing as a divine sign. Relations with other people, whether individually or collectively, and with the world, both as a totality and as an infinity of signs, are determined by the vertical axis connecting the core of human selfhood and God as Peace. This upright path is open to everyone, and only on it can we tease out and resolve the differences and tensions associated with every path in the project of life. The individual who prays to God by addressing Him as Thou does so in the name of us all. Albeit as an individual, each of us prays of our own free will for everyone. Traveling on the upright path leads to the encounter with or discovery of human being in original and sublime uprightness. With and through this goal, one discovers and realizes beauty of character.

What we experience in the external world as jewish, christian, or muslim, for example, may be explained or understood only if we accept that everything in existence reveals the one same God, but that He never shows the same aspect two moments in a row. As Abū Tālib al-Makkī says, "God never discloses Himself in a single form to two different individuals, nor in a single form twice."[16] Connection to God and the upright path are open to everyone regardless of what group they belong to. With this connection, differences can be explained. Without it, they cannot. Those who try to stay on the upright path put up with incomprehensible differences and search for a way to establish relationships with others and with the different by opening up toward the One:

> Call thou to the way of thy Lord
> with wisdom and good admonition,
> and dispute with them in the better way.

> Surely thy Lord knows very well those
> who have gone astray from His way,
> and He knows very well those who are guided.[17]

3. THE STRANGER

As individuals, each of us is in relation with him- or herself, the countless multitude of other persons, and the world as a whole, which is made up of an indeterminable diversity of phenomena and levels of being. Both the individual and everyone together are, like the world as a whole, a revelation of Unity. He is their inner core. Each of us, however, is cut off from the One, both recollecting and forgetting Him through the countless multitude of signs in both outer and inner worlds.

Our relationship to ourselves involves a split between body and Spirit, whose relations change from moment to moment. Total ascendancy of the body is the lowest level of human existence, while total ascendancy of Spirit is the realization of humanity in perfected creaturehood, the revelation of Spirit in the self, and the return to Peace. But it should at once be stressed that Spirit is not subject to our limited will. It submits only to God's will.

We exist in relation to other people as well. These relationships shape our sense-of-self. The closeness and remoteness of bodies and tongues, signs and meaning, fears and hopes, kinship and foreignness, doctrine and ritual all play their parts. Closeness and remoteness determine the boundaries at which the way in which the sense-of-self is formed changes, where it stops and/or starts. But neither closeness nor remoteness can be so established as to last without change. Each of these relations contains irreducible difference. Closeness can be desirable and tolerable or hateful and intolerable, as can remoteness. So long as difference is considered in purely quantitative terms, it is irreducible. It remains irreducible until we recognize our own potential for realizing the best qualities. Each of us is the possibility of such realization. No matter how far we have come, this possibility is never exhausted. Our prayer to God that He guide us on the upright path is nothing other than acceptance of this openness and a move toward it.

Adopting this openness toward the Perfection manifest in the countless levels of existence, whatever our position, we can conceive of and accept what is other and different as always already known to the All-Knowing, connected to Him in a fundamental way and always before Him.

In our prayer to God for guidance on the upright path, we learn of vertical axes in both human being and in the world. The axis in human being proceeds from the darkness of our deepest depth to the light of the Spirit. The relation of these two extremes and the form they take in self-being are our condition. We can rise out of this condition or fall below it. We may remain in one and the same condition for some time, but not forever. Awareness that the condition of the self is subject to change stimulates remembrance to fulfill its potential through witness to the One as the foundation and goal of our journey and quest. Only by witness to the One can human being raise itself from a lower to a higher level and become a traveler on the upright path. Wherever we may be on that path, our knowledge has sense only through recognition of Mystery. We can never know everything, nor can we fail to be fully known by Him to Whom we turn. This is why not knowing is at the same time recognition that the unknowability of God conditions all our knowledge: "The eyes attain Him not, but He attains the eyes."[1]

Like that vertical axis within human being, from the darkness of the body to the light of the Spirit, another vertical axis runs from earth to heaven. Everything on earth, in heaven, and in between gathers in our body and Spirit and whatever is between them.

The upright path of the outer world runs from earth to heaven and signifies Intellect. Regardless of how far removed from the Principle things may be, they remain always connected with the Real through Intellect. Given that our realization takes place in the Spirit, which is a form of the manifestation of Intellect, the self's return to Peace, its lost home, reveals both the stations of the self and the world as alien territory in which we are but sojourners, our Master's guests.

That the difference between individual phenomena cannot be judged, in the full meaning of that term, indicates that it is in that difference that God is revealed as always other. He is thus both remote and close to everything. The impossibility of human judgment regarding difference recognizes God as absolute otherness. Only thus can one explain how God is at once close and remote, similar and incomparable, or that the infinite moment and the point are the principles of all time and all space while also always both in and outside them.

The question of the other or the stranger is a crucial one for human righteousness and for recognition of the truth in every phenomenon and acceptance of its indelibility from everything in either the external or inner world. That God is (the) other to all existence allows the recognition and crossing of the boundaries that determine everything in existence.

When we transgress the boundaries of group or individual sense-of-self, we consider ourselves strangers, as do others. That this boundary can be crossed determines both individual and group sense-of-self. Only consciousness of the stranger allows boundaries to be determined. Without it, they would have no meaning.

Strangers are the incarnation of the unknown. They are from some other country, with some other language, customs, beliefs and rituals, and so forth. Most of these differences are irreducible. The stranger is a particular seen in its fullness. One can get to know the stranger and even get used to him or her. But the strangers never lose their particularity. In the case of the stranger it becomes clear that all individuals and all peoples are strangers and that this fact conditions the sense-of-self.

The distinction between "us," on the one hand, and "them" as strangers, on the other, cannot excuse excluding or ignoring the distinction between "amongst us" and "amongst them." Instruction always comes "amongst us" in our language. This is as true for them as for us:

> We have sent no Messenger save with the tongue of his people, that he might make all clear to them.[2]

Every prophet received and transmitted the Revelation in the tongue of his people. As the essence of each Revelation, namely our eternal debt to God,[3] is always the same, it may be expressed in any tongue, even though originally revealed in only one tongue. This means that Revelation may be translated from one tongue to all others. The essence of prophecy is to draw attention to the One as our innermost core and the source of our humanity. Every prophet has spoken of the One, always in the tongue of those around him. The Prophet Muhammad, however, was sent to all people.[4] The Revelation to him is in Arabic. Viewed from the perspective of other peoples, he and the Revelation are strangers. It is only by translation that one can reconcile the facts that the Prophet was an Arab and the Recitation was in Arabic, but that they were sent to all people, to whom the Prophet was a stranger and the Revelation incomprehensible. The Arab can have no advantage over the foreigner, nor the foreigner over the Arab.[5] The presence of the Recitation in every tongue allows those who hearken to it to be singled out, particularly with regard to their consciousness of God:

> If We had sent it down on a stranger and he had recited it to them, they would not have believed in it.[6]

Only by seeing every individual and everything around us as signs of the One can we respond to the stranger. In contact with the unknown and the stranger, one can decipher the mystery only insofar as one accepts that the stranger is known by the Creator Who is equally close to all. The stranger is always seen through misted glass, as our knowledge is limited and conditioned. Something may seem good to us, which is not. And the reverse.[7] Only God knows all. If we were to see with God's eye, then we would be able to judge the stranger in his or her wholeness. To attempt this is to take one's passions for a god.[8] And that is unforgivable sin. Relationship with the stranger means to encounter oneself in relation to an unknown possibility. In that encounter, questions of tolerance and of difference take on crucial importance.

To say "I" or "I am" always means and says "not-I" and "I am not." This is because I begins or ends at the boundary with not-I. The dignity of an I cannot be separated from what it defines as not-I. Human dignity, which is to say spirituality, corporeality, and belonging to society, is impossible without this boundary. It cannot be crossed by strangers. The stranger or other determines the boundary and so dignity. If "I am" were determined only in relation to the stranger or "I am not" and not also in relation to the Absolute, then "I am not" would determine the sense-of-self. This would deny that "Our God and your God is One."[9] "I am" and "I am not" relate to one and the same God. Both are within society or societies. They may share the same or use different linguistic, symbolic, and semantic systems to form and express their senses-of-self and connection with the outer world. If these systems are different, then the nature of the stranger is determined by that difference.

Our attempt to live and be happy *forever* introduces into our existence the question of deliverance or Peace. That means that we are seekers after Peace. The relationship with what we seek is seeking or quest. But we cannot find the Peace we seek unless we admit He is always more than we are and that we must free ourselves from associating to Him anything He is not. Not to accept that means denying the possibility of shifting our sense-of-self from lower to higher levels of being. To accept it means submitting to it as greater. The more determined the quest, the greater the role of the Quarry becomes, the less that of the seeker. Finally, the Quarry will express Himself entirely in the seeker: "And if one comes one span nearer to Me, I go one cubit nearer to him."[10]

Such a final result means that the seeker recognizes each phenomenon and accords it its rights, as the Prophet says, "You should give the rights of all those who have a right on you."[11] To accord their rights to all means to live in justice, if only on one's own account. Justice is to speak and show the truth. There is nothing which was not created with truth. Therefore, one must recognize the truth and right in whatever is another's, strange, or different. Confessing the truth and giving right are fundamental principles. They appear in every sign in a different way. Knowledge of the world is reached by reading its signs. They are inscriptions of the Creator. He who reads them is a transcription of that inscription. The Creator has revealed to him the Book which is the inscription of both—the world and human being—but in fullness of speech. This Book is, like human being and the world, divine speech. He reveals Himself to people through it too. Thus God's speech acts in human speech, but they are not to be reduced to each other.

For us to be clear that God is truth, the stranger must exist. Recognizing this, we confirm that we can find the Quarry only as a stranger, as only through the stranger is sense-of-self possible. Denying the stranger means denying the truth. And the reverse: Recognizing the stranger means recognizing the truth. Given that the truth always appears in a form that confines the "I am" and from which it seeks release, it is important to see that these boundaries are determined by difference and the many and that they are constantly changing. That is the meaning of God's will:

> O mankind, We have created you male and female,
> and appointed you races and tribes,
> that you may know one another.
> Surely the noblest among you in the sight of
> God is the most conscious of you.
> All-knowing, All-aware.[12]

> To every one of you
> We have appointed a right way and an open road.
> If God had willed, He would have made you

one nation; but that He may try you
in what has come to you. So be you forward
in good works; unto God shall you return,
all together; and He will tell you of that
whereon you were at variance.[13]

4. SELF-KNOWLEDGE

Our highest faculty is self-knowledge. This knowledge always meets its limit in the other or stranger. Knowing oneself entails knowledge of the other. But to know oneself also means to redeem oneself (through self-realization). This is possible only through transgression of that limit and redeeming the other (by bringing about this self-realization). The other cannot, however, be confined to the great chain of being. Preoccupied with ourselves, we are led to questions about the self, the body, and society. The question of the self cannot be answered by neglecting its corporeal expression. But, just like the self as a whole, corporeality is conditioned by various levels of society—family, one's native community, one's people, and humanity in all its diversity.

Humanity is part of the terrestrial whole shaped by interaction with heaven. Whether traveling away from ourselves toward heaven or the reverse, we face ultimate questions. Ignoring them or putting them to one side prevents us from seeing the reasons for otherness. And without that, we cannot know or realize ourselves. Redeeming or realizing the self requires recognition that redemption (and self-realization) is equally important for others—Jews, Christians, Sabaeans, and so forth. For the question of our own redemption to receive a positive response, so must that of others:

Surely they that believe, and those of Jewry, and Sabaeans, and
those Christians, whosoever believes in God and the Last Day,
and works righteousness—no fear shall be on them, neither
shall they sorrow.[1]

As the verses make clear, being nominally Jewish, Christian, or
Sabaean—and these names are just examples—is not and cannot be
enough for redemption. Individual redemption requires faith in God,
judgment, and the doing of good deeds. Differences due to religious
identification neither prevent nor guarantee redemption. Full humanity may be realized through any of these identifications. This is not on
the basis of identification but on the grounds of humanity. At the core
of any individual, in our deepest nature, is confession of divine Unity.
We are not that Unity, however. That is why we stand between the
remembrance and the forgetting of Him. The meaning of the variety
of human existence fades when it stops reminding us of our defining
nature.

The Last Day is required so that differences with regard to the
stranger and the other may be explained. Self-knowledge entails the
stranger, but the difference involved can be determined only by the
One. The essence of the revelation to the Prophet after his Ascent to
the Lotus of the furthest boundary[2] is his bringing together of all difference in his transcription of the divine word (his life and teaching).
Through his ascent, he reached the furthest boundary or sublime
closeness with God. He realized or discovered his authentic perfection. His being was empty of any will except God's. Through return
to God, the Prophet gathered all the possibilities of human being—
from the sevenfold circumambulation of the House in the Valley to the
seven heavens and sublime closeness to God. Beyond the boundary is
the Mystery. This experience revealed to the Prophet what many consider the heart of being-at-peace:

> The Messenger believes in what was sent down to him from his
> Lord, and the believers; each one believes in God and His
> angels, and in His Books and His Messengers; we make no divi-
> sion between any one of His Messengers. They say, "We hear,

and obey. Our Lord, grant us Thy forgiveness; unto Thee is the homecoming."[3]

For us to know ourselves as human beings, we must come to terms with the linguistic, symbolic, and semantic systems that condition our sense-of-self. Recognizing this in ourselves, we affirm the same of the other and the different. To accept all the messengers is to confess that although they are different, the essence of what they have revealed is one and the same. We turn to this essence through signs in the world, other people, and ourselves: "And of His signs is the creation of the heavens and earth and the variety of your tongues and hues."[4] Thus, we find ourselves recognizing that both sense-of-self and non-self are statements in (different) linguistic, symbolic, and semantic systems under one God and so mutually translatable, so that mutual knowledge is possible. Only those who recognize a sacred dignity in the other's difference may come to know each other. The appearance of signs in the world and the self, which make clear that He is the truth, leads us onto the path of self-knowledge and knowledge of the Lord, as there is no otherness to which He is not privy. He alone is Other to everything. Relationship to the other and the different entails relationship to God as the Creator of everything. When the divine presence is excluded from this relationship, it becomes covering of or association with Him (idolatry). Covering God means forming a false idea of God and seeing in Him what is not there and should not be imputed to Him. Association with God is idolatry, making something or someone equivalent to God and attributing to it that authority and primacy which in truth belongs to God alone. It includes any case of establishing an authority or value as independent of God or of misrecognizing it as autonomous rather than derived. In such cases, we have taken our own power of judgment for sufficient and descend into hostility toward and conspiracy with people.

But signs in the world and the self are always both clear and unclear. Accordingly, human beings can never make final judgments. Our knowledge is never final. If we prejudge on the basis of our little knowledge, we assign meaning to signs, ignoring obscurities and failing to recognize our finite nature and the possibility of return from it to Fullness or the Absolute. In this way, human being takes passions and thoughts for God. What we take for clarity is never without obscurity. The simple fact of the descent of the world and the Book means that truth resides with them, but not that they are truth itself. In the Recitation, the Highest explains it as follows:

It is He who sent down upon thee the Book, wherein are verses clear that are the Essence of the Book, and others ambiguous. As for those in whose hearts is swerving, they follow the ambiguous part, desiring dissension, and desiring its interpretation; and none knows its interpretation, save only God. And those firmly rooted in knowledge say, "We believe in it; all is from our Lord"; yet none remembers, but men possessed of minds.[5]

The acceptance of human creaturehood cannot be divorced from recognition of the world as God's revelation, and that means confessing that there is no real except the Real. We always have two paths open to us—toward the Real and toward void. Recognition that signs in the world and the self abide with the Real allows us to distinguish the false from the true, the forbidden from the allowed. That is innate in our nature, and we thereby recognize that all existence proceeds from and returns to God. The Prophet says:

Both legal and illegal things are obvious and in between them are doubtful matters. So whoever forsakes those doubtful things lest he may commit a sin, will definitely avoid what is clearly illegal; and whoever indulges in these doubtful things bravely, is likely to commit what is clearly illegal.[6]

Unclear signs may be interpreted only through clear ones. Confessing belief in God and His angels, His books, and His prophets and messengers, without singling out any of those things, is to recognize His remoteness and closeness to every human being and that the legacy of all of His messengers is common to all, albeit expressed in different linguistic, symbolic, and semantic systems. The differences may be bridged by faith and reliance on the common essence of their spoken discourses. Given that each discourse is set down in a written record, each of them unfolds the revelation of Unity.

When we encounter the other or the different, as a community with a common language, we experience them as negating our self-understanding. But the other and the different do not abrogate the sense-of-self; loss of connection with truth, becoming unjust, and, most of all, taking one's own passions for God do. Truth and justice are not entirely on one side. When human being experiences injustice from *that* side of the boundary, this introduces us to the world's double nature, allowing us to strengthen our allegiance to justice and bear witness before all. In the Recitation, God has revealed that the other and the different also partake of dignity through witness to justice. Relationship and friendship with the other and the different are not based on linguistic, symbolic, or semantic systems. Injustice at the hands of the other provides us, as interlocutors, an opportunity to recognize our own potential for injustice and to requite it with fairness. The presence of justice amongst them enables us to see that God is always and everywhere Other and to see the path of realization or return in our experience of whatever is in the world: "Every soul shall taste of death; and We try you with evil and good for a testing, then unto Us you shall be returned."[7]

That is why justice may be demanded for jews, christians, and sabaeans. Relationship to the other and the different requires one to love them even if it seems unrequited: "You love them, and they love you not."[8] In this way, one recognizes that God's mercy is all encompassing. This takes the form of the constant and unconditional doing of good deeds.[9] And that, furthermore, means that it is possible within every community to distinguish true from false and to adhere to the true, recognizing it in everything.[10] Relations with people may include or deny confession of the true in everything, which is justice. But denial is contrary to our ability for self-realization in and with truth. That is the meaning of God's call:

> O believers, be you securers of justice, witnesses for God, even
> though it be against yourselves, or your parents and kinsmen,

whether the man be rich or poor; God stands closest to either.
Then follow not caprice, so as to swerve.[11]

The call for unconditional witness of justice cannot be separated
from the command "for you will love them." Love in its original fullness requires no response. When one encounters the other as cause of
love, one should persevere regardless of response or whether one
meets with resistance, lack of interest, injustice, and so forth. The response will not alter the witness of one who accepts justice and loves
the other because the primary grounds are found in them (and not the
response).

Relationship with the stranger is relationship with God. Wherever
we turn, we encounter the divine Face.[12] Every relationship with the
other involves the Face turning toward us. Failure to recognize the
presence of divine mercy in the face of the other is denial of His signs.
Being-at-peace is everywhere and always possible, given the recognition of God as the absolute Other and acceptance that comes through
other people and the world in general: "My face has found peace in
God."[13]

Humankind is the culmination of all creation. We gather in ourselves everything created before us. We alone experience both fullness
and unity with our whole being. The creation is in seven heavens and
ages. So is human being. Our sense-of-self reflects these seven levels.
When the Self sent down the Book to humanity, it brought explanation of everything that is in all of existence, that it might be said in
human language. The Book thus belongs to both the external world
with its seven heavens and to our inner world, whose fullness is also
distributed on seven levels:

> Believers, God has sent down to you, for a remembrance, a
> Messenger reciting to you the signs of God, clear signs, that He
> may bring forth those who believe and do righteous deeds from
> the shadows into the light. Whosoever believes in God and does
> righteousness, He will admit him to gardens underneath which
> rivers flow; therein they shall dwell for ever and ever. God has
> made for him a goodly provision.

It is God who created seven heavens, and of earth their like,
between them the Command descending, that you may know
that God is powerful over everything and that God encompasses
everything in knowledge.[14]

The creation of the seven heavens involves emanation from God's
own Self to ours, and God says, "I have sent down."[15] His "I," however, reveals Him through His most beautiful names and says, "We
have sent down."[16] The beautiful names exist in fallen humanity's
sense-of-self as a possibility to be realized in perfect human being. If
we do bring any of God's beautiful attributes to realization in character, we secure return to the Garden, which is to say our original and
authentic condition. Given that our sense-of-self is the culmination of
all existence, sublime potential links us to Unity through the Holy
Spirit:

> Say, "The Holy Spirit sent it down from thy Lord
> in truth, and to confirm those who believe,
> and to be a guidance and good tidings
> to those who choose peace."[17]

5. THE SENSE-OF-SELF AND THE DEBT

Islam is the key word in every muslim's identity. It signifies a religious doctrine, its impact on history, and its potential future influence. That is how the term is used for the most part today, although its original (and authentic) meaning refers to our relationship with transcendent beginning and end.

As is always the case with human identities and the associated terminology, this all-comprehensive name seems close to us because muslims use it as the keyword of their existence. It also seems remote because others often use it in a way entirely opposed to the feelings and beliefs of muslims. The name is thus to be found in the feelings and understanding both of those who use it to mark the other and encounters with the other through history and of those who use it to designate their own identity and their highest aspirations. Both uses involve contradictions deserving of attention, as the best way to see through something is to investigate it for contradictions.

To clarify for both muslims and others the role of the term *islam* in the complex of doctrine, ritual, and virtue to which muslims endeavor to belong, we may look at the tradition (*hadith*) that opens the *Sahih Muslim*, one of the best known collections of the Prophet Muhammad's sayings, acts, and opinions. (This collection of the traditions of the Prophet Muhammad, together with six similar collections and the *Qur'an*, form the textual basis of the overall teaching commonly called *islam*.)

This textual heritage is decisive for the formation of the sense-of-self of both individuals and groups who designate themselves as muslim. God or His messenger speaks in them. The texts are thus the expression of God and His messenger as speakers. He who would know of God and His messenger should turn to these discourses. Since their appearance in history, a temporal current has been established in which they and their interpretation have been transmitted and developed. Interpretation communities, which include the texts and previous approaches to them, have come into being. Although interpretation of the Recitation and of the sayings of the Prophet has gone on for more than fourteen centuries, it remains an inexhaustible (re)source for every muslim's attempt to realize the self in virtue through ritual and doctrine based on these discourses and for which they provide the essential content.

These texts are unchanging in their literal content, but interpretation varies from individual to individual and from interpretation community to interpretation community. This is because interpretation reflects the relationship between unchanging text and conditioned or finite sense-of-self, which is subject to change from moment to moment.[1] The conditioned self cannot affect the text, but the text may affect the sense-of-self. Whenever the sense-of-self adopts itself as measure and criterion of the relationship to the text, it reads into it its own finitude and finds that instead of the text. That is violence, distortion, and alteration of the text, which, as divine discourse, is sacred. When we take our passions for our God,[2] which is what this violence to the text is, the result is distortion of our authentic nature and heedless falling ever lower.[3] This fall involves separation from the Principle and approach to void.

Disagreements in interpretation are common, and they sustain the flow of discussion, with none of the participants able to lay claim to final judgment. Whenever final judgment is attempted in discussion, the decisive role of differences, which are always with God, is denied.

Whatever the relationship between the self and the Text and whatever it results in, the self's knowledge remains little. No self can lay claim to full knowledge or final judgment. Should it try, it merely denies that divine knowledge is all-encompassing,[4] that the spirit is at the Lord's bidding,[5] that it bloweth where He listeth,[6] that man is poor,[7] and that he is given only a little knowledge.[8]

The Recitation is the key text in forming the sense-of-self in relation to God. For the muslim, it is God's discourse as revealed to men through the Prophet Muhammad. To the Prophet, it was his first command. Receiving and testifying to it, he shaped his sense-of-self entirely in accordance with it. The Recitation became his nature.[9] That is why, according to the Recitation, he is the best example for those to whom he delivered it. The traditions collected in the books provide testimony of the Prophet's nature.

The tradition given below brings together and reveals the meanings of the key terms of the Recitation and the relationships between them: being-at-peace (*islam*), faith (*iman*), beauty or the good (*ihsan*), and the hour (*sa'a*) as key components of our debt to God (*din*).

'Umar ibn al-Khattab said, "One day when we were with God's Messenger, a man with very white clothing and very black hair came up to us. No mark of travel was visible on him, and none of us recognized him. Sitting down before the Prophet, leaning his knees against his, and placing his hands on his thighs, he said, "Tell me, Muhammad, about being-at-peace."

He replied, "Being-at-peace means that you should bear witness that there is no god but God and that Muhammad is God's messenger, that you should perform the ritual prayer, pay the alms tax, fast during Ramadan, and make the pilgrimage to the House if you are able to go there."

The man said, "You have spoken the truth." We were surprised at his questioning him and then declaring that he had spoken the truth. He said, "Now tell me about faith."

He replied, "Faith means that you have faith in God, His angels, His books, His messengers, and the Last Day, and that you have faith in the measuring out, both its good and its evil."

Remarking that he had spoken the truth, he then said, "Now tell me about doing what is beautiful."

He replied, "Doing what is beautiful means that you should worship God as if you see Him, for even if you do not see Him, He sees you."

Then the man said, "Tell me about the Hour."

The Prophet replied, "About that he who is questioned knows no more than the questioner."

The man said, "Then, tell me about its marks."

He said, "The slave girl will give birth to her mistress, and you will see the barefoot, the naked, the destitute, and the shepherds vying with each other in building."

Then the man went away. After I had waited for a long time, the Prophet said to me, "Do you know who the questioner was, 'Umar?" I replied, "God and His messenger know the best." He said, "He was Gabriel.[10] He came to teach you your Debt."[11]

The very form of this tradition testifies to the nature of muslim doctrine, ritual, and virtue. The entire event takes place in the presence of a group gathered around the Prophet Muhammad. By the call he sent to people, God chose him as his messenger and revealed or sent down to him knowledge of the origin, condition, and future of the world and of humanity through the Angel Gabriel. He passed on this call to us, after first making his own peace with it. He passed on that through which he realized his own self. What he had received became his nature, and he is accordingly the best example of witness to it.

The Prophet Muhammad is not then the source of what he said. His human nature received and related. His humanity was chosen and formed for what the Creator revealed to him, His creature and servant even before His messenger. He accepted the Angel Gabriel as the bearer of the message and news from God. For God is Peace, as He says Himself.[12] Bonding with Him as Peace, the Prophet accepted the command to be first of the people-of-peace.[13]

The Prophet Muhammad accepted the message, became first of the people-of-peace, spoke out what he had received, and bore witness through his discourse and manner of life. It is up to us, on the basis of our free will, to accept or reject. The choice is ours, as are the consequences. The Prophet did not claim to bring new doctrine, only a new revelation of one and the same lesson that all God's prophets have received, related, and born witness to. Its essence is the confession of God's Unity as the most profound content of humanity. The lesson allows us to find or discover in our character our full potential and it does so by discovering our authentic nature and reforming our sense-of-self after God's call. The Prophet Muhammad is the best example. His character was powerful[14] and the most beautiful divine names came to realization in his sense-of-self. Through this process of realization, we rediscover ourselves as made in God's image and true uprightness.

But the Prophet Muhammad, like every other Prophet before him, broke in all he said and did with the content and form of the inherited order, in which, to lesser or greater degree, consciousness and confession of Unity had waned. He called on people to join him in this. For him, the only valid order and way of behavior was that which confirms God in His revelation. He pointed to an order founded on the acceptance of gods other than God, in which authentic human nature was covered and subjected to these gods. He pricked the conscience of humanity by reminding us of our authentic nature, which is designed to bear witness that there is no god but God. So a new order begins with the Prophet Muhammad, and the existing is weighed, confirmed, or rejected. This new order is the revelation of authentic humanity, manifest in everything—in the self and in the world—just as everything is manifest in it. It is the recognition of right in all.

Muhammad or, to translate his name, the Praised was the perfect human being, a light and an example. In him, as the perfect human being, everything revealed in all creation is gathered. God is the Unity all the worlds reveal. The worlds of creation praise their creator and are praised in their wholeness. They have received praise from God, and they express it by praising Him. Humanity is the culmination of creation. Everything dispersed in all existence is gathered in us. Our essence is unity, realized in the signs within the self, which praise God both individually and collectively.

So, the world as a whole expresses praise to God, the Lord of the worlds, and is thus a praiser. So do we, at our best. Muhammad is the realization of this best. His entire being expressed praise to God the Lord of the worlds. This human perfection, expressed by his being Praised and Praiser, is the essence of each one of us too. Self-realization is bonding with the Praised, taking him for a model, and approximating to him. The more we realize the nature of the Praised in our innermost self, the closer we are to him. Muhammad's discourse revealed unity in human language and being. It is therefore understandable how the Praised/Praiser epitomizes all of creation, from beginning to end.

Because of our finite nature, the following question is crucial for each and every one of us: What is it that we have and from where? If we want a final answer to this question, our search will tell us that we have nothing we did not receive from the Creator. We have received both ourselves and everything we do and are in debt to the One who has given it to us. In this way, we are debtors of the Creator through the Debt. Recognition of this relationship requires an answer to the further question of the Nature of the Debt. Why has the Creator given His creatures a form of earth and why did He breathe His Spirit into us? What is the relationship between God as the Real, on the one hand, and human being and the world, as IIis revelation, on the other?

These questions must be answered if we are to determine our potential relationship with the world and God. The relationship covers the entire span of human selfhood, from the lowest level to authentic perfection, from a given human being to every other human being in the same and every other time, from our immediate environment to the furthest reaches. For us to answer the question of the Debt to the Creator, we must recognize the boundaries between the countless levels of existence. They start from our desire to realize peace within ourselves and in that peace and from it to attain knowledge of the One, and to love Him as our most profound nature, with which we wish to be at one. And given that we are always in the conditioned or finite, what we yearn for appears to us in the form of Beauty. In this way, we steadily withdraw from illusion and approach the Hour, as the Real in us where the sense-of-self dwells. Desiring to know the sense-of-self, we liberate ourselves from appearances, which is to say everything that is outside the Hour. And the Hour, in its fullness, is what enables all existence: Everything is of It and returns to It.

6. Being-at-Peace

Each of us is, as such, life, consciousness, will, power, and speech. But not that alone. We are much more, but nevertheless remain between void and the Absolute. Our life, consciousness, will, power, and discourse are conditioned. In them, their opposites are also revealed— death, unconsciousness, the unwilled, impotence, and speechlessness. These attributes belong absolutely to God alone, so that there is no life but Life, no consciousness but Consciousness, no will but Will, no power but Power, no speech but Speech. Existence is the revelation of the One. It is an infinite multitude of signs which all speak of the One.

Everything in existence, from earth to heaven, gathers and is revealed in the human sense of self—body and spirit. And all that is oriented in infinite ways toward either the Absolute or void. In the ceaseless flux on the path between these two, the self seeks Peace. No matter how close it comes to Peace, the danger of forgetting remains. It never ceases to be between ascent and falling. Once kindled, the desire for Peace never ceases. Whatever our condition, God remains both close and remote, merciful and severe.

Every human being is a relationship to Peace, as a seeker of Peace or person-of-peace. Being-at-peace is the relationship of the person-of-peace to Peace as the divine presence in us. We realize ourselves in

Mercy and closeness to the Principle. This relationship may be presented in an infinite number of linguistic, symbolic, and semantic systems without betraying its essence. Being-at-peace is humanity, and vice versa. It is impossible to attain a condition where human poverty and dependence cease, however. Through being-at-peace as our relationship to Peace, we realize our indebtedness to the Creator as source and sanctuary of all humanity. As human, we are pre-adapted for that realization. It is our highest possibility. That pre-adaptation is our core or authentic nature. It is our original covenant with the Lord, our innermost nature. The human capacity to attain perfection never fades, for our essence is sacred. It is the Creator's will translated to His creatures, His constant closeness to them. With reference to this "highest possibility," one must stress it comes to realization through "the beautiful names." There are many names, but they are all most beautiful. This is why one may say of the many expressions of human capacity that they are all "the highest." None of them is that, however, unless it involves return to God as the One, Who is both near and far.

The proof of our capacity lies in the perfect—the prophets and the good, who are infinite in number. Their common essence is orientation toward Peace, which renders them peaceful and their way being-at-peace. They are always of a language and time, but never dependent upon them. Time and place are for them opportunities for revelation of the One, nothing else. They are simultaneously connected to the One by His closeness and separated from Him by His remoteness. The limits of their sense-of-self confirm limitlessness and their being involves full recognition of the boundary. Their desire is to learn the limits that reveal the Mystery, which can be known only by recognizing that it cannot be known. They belong to a ritual that confirms the irreducibility of the difference between any two things in existence. This ritual is the eternal repetition of speech out of silence and the reverse, of going and returning, of dividing and joining.

Being-at-peace is defined in the first answer to the Angel Gabriel's questioning. It is our willing response to the message the Prophet Muhammad brought as God's call. The message is delivered to each individual in intelligible form. The Prophet Muhammad is the foremost and most beautiful example of human being accepting and following the call. Each one of us to whom the call has come faces an intelligible choice between acceptance and rejection. Acceptance means freely confessing that there is no god but God and that Muhammad is His Messenger.

This confession has two parts. In the first, the Unity of God is affirmed through the ellipsis that "there is no god but God" (*la ilāha illāllāh*), and by denying that anything in the external world or in human interiority may be a self-sufficient cause. The world as a whole is, therefore, just the revelation of God, but it is not God. In this witness to Unity, the whole of existence is ordered from above, from the Principle, downward, so that all the worlds and all the things in them partake of the nature of divine signs. They are nothing outside of the One.

The second part stresses that the totality of the world as revelation of God is caught and gathered in human perfection or the boundless praise of God. The fullness of such praise is Muhammad. As such, he was chosen and sent to us to reveal our highest potential—the pure praising of God.

Praising God is the essence of Muhammad both as human being and prophet. Everything that is created manifests praise of God. Accordingly, Muhammad's essence is in the very act of creation: There is nothing that does not praise the Creator. Muhammad is also the last in a long line of prophets of one and the same God, gathering in themselves and presenting one and the same essence of the praise of God. What Muhammad reveals is essentially what all the other prophets of the same God revealed, all 124,000 of them, including Adam, Noah, Abraham, Ishmael, Isaac, Jacob, Joseph, Moses, Aaron, David, Solomon, John, and Jesus.

This witness and both its parts define in language the relationship of one who accepts it as a person-of-peace (*muslim*) to God as Peace (*al-Salām*).[1] Peace is the highest principle and is present in all of creation. Being recipient and conduit, in calm and peacefulness, is the existential form of relation to the Principle.[2] Human character is formed through receiving and giving, but always in the context of our nature as created and indebted. We can realize beauty of character only as peaceful beings who receive and give, suffer and act, listen and respond, always in relation to the Highest Principle. The person-of-peace's relationship of being-at-peace in Peace determines his or her actions, existence, and appearance in the totality of the world, but always in relation to God.[3] Given that the call of Peace was sent to all being as well as to all the spheres of voluntary human existence, additional proof of witness is required.

While the first element of being-at-peace is confessing that there is no god but God and that the Praised is His servant and His messenger, there are four further proofs.

The second proof of being-at-peace is prayer. We are called to make the regulated prayer five times a day, at particular times. This may be done at any place, but always turned toward the House or the Sacred Mosque[4] in the Valley of Bekka. It involves preparatory cleansing with water or clean earth, followed by the utterance, aloud or to oneself, of formulae and excerpts from the Recitation in the way of the Prophet. This includes certain postures and movements, from standing through bowing to prostration and finally sitting and moving the head right and left while saying "peace" (*salām*). When beginning to pray, the person-of-peace accepts the Ka'ba as representing the common focus of all humankind. In this way, all existence is reduced to the duality of the human subject and the external world. Given that the core or essence of everything is one and the same, through prayer human being seeks to unify the internal and the external essences, which is to confess that there is no god but God.

The third proof of being-at-peace is the giving of purificatory alms (*zakat*). Given that our cause lies entirely in an external will, our individuality cannot be reduced to ourselves alone. Every form of greed or feeling of sufficiency is a denial of authentic nature. That authentic nature is pure and inscribed within our origin and end. To prevent our reducing our existence to ourselves alone, we must bear witness by giving of everything we have that appears to us proof of independence. By so giving, we connect with the other. These others are the weak and sick, foreigners or travelers, anyone the giver seems more powerful than but who is in principle just as important in the world: they are our brothers in Debt and companions in creaturehood.[5] By giving, we show consciousness of having received mercy ourselves. The giver channels this mercy into our relationship with the other.

The fourth proof of being-at-peace is fasting during the month of Ramadan. Given our dependence on the external world and our connection to it, the patterns of our links to food and other people begin to appear valuable in themselves, independent of the final cause and consequence. To shift focus toward the ultimate cause of things, including pleasure in food and drink and sexual relations, abstention is enjoined as a form of witness. The focus shifts toward confession that there is no god but God and that there is no cause but the Cause. The time of fasting is determined by the position of the earth with regard to the sun and the lunar changes. Our voluntary acquiescence to the Call produces a harmony of change throughout existence. Sensible of dependence on food, we create relations with the world that mislead us in a false covenant whereby we strengthen our own independence. By fasting, we turn to God as the Independent and try to shape ourselves after that name and to realize authentic poverty.[6]

The fifth proof is the journey to the House in the Valley of Bekka. The House is the center of the Valley, and its environs are blessed. In that holy place, at certain times of the lunar year, rituals are prescribed of visitation and pilgrimage (*hajj*). The House (*al-bayt*) or the Sacred Mosque (*al-masjid al-haram*) was raised or, so the oldest sources say, sent down at the time when Adam, the first man and first prophet of God, came to Earth from Paradise (*jannah*). The Mosque is at the bottom of the Valley. It marks our fall from the condition of paradise or beautiful righteousness to the lowest level. During that fall, Adam's turn or return to God took place. That is the significance of the Ka'ba, the simplest form of building where we turned to begin our ascent to the Furthest Mosque. Ascent to the Furthest Mosque represents the rediscovery of our authentic nature—being perfect in relation to God as Peace. God's calls to His other prophets and their responses are connected with the Sacred Mosque. Particular stress is placed on the prophet Abraham and his son Ishmael, as direct ancestors of the Prophet Muhammad.

The House marks the center of all existence. Humankind is like an emanation that proceeds from that center, outside place and time, but also like a circle around it. We are always close to the One and far from Him. The human heart is the image of that House in the self. The attempt to bring into harmony the center of human interiority and the center of the external world is nothing other than affirmation of witness as part of the community of those who have responded to the divine call sent through the Prophet Muhammad. The seven circumambulations of the House correspond to the seven days of creation and the seven heavens. By turning to it, prostrating oneself before it, and passing around it, we realize the unity of the external world and our inner nature.

The House is shaped like a cube (*ka'ba*). It is the center of the Sacred Mosque, at the bottom of the Valley of Tears. As such, it signifies our situation at the bottom of a descending arc: existence as the revelation of divine Unity begins in the Intellect, through which the divine Names are revealed, and it comes to an end in us. In that end place or being-in-the-depths, we gather what is dispersed throughout the external world. The Ka'ba signifies the possibility of recoiling from that extreme and beginning the ascent or return to the One. This return is human self-realization as signified by Muhammad's Nocturnal Ascent. The Ascent starts at the Sacred Mosque at the bottom of the Valley, which signifies the extremity of our fall and contact with void. At the end is our self-realization in Intellect and the return to Unity, signified by the Furthest Mosque on Temple Mount. The Prophet Muhammad traverses the way from lowest to highest in one night, as God says in the Recitation:

> Glory be to Him, Who carried His Servant by night from the Sacred Mosque to the Furthest Mosque, the precincts of which We have blessed that We might show him some of Our Signs: He is the All-hearing, the All-seeing.[7]

All the forms of being-at-peace listed earlier—confessing Unity, prayer, giving, fasting, and pilgrimage—are acts of individual free will. No one can be forced to them. This is because human will is present in each of them, as a response to God's call. The goal of being-at-peace is to bring these two wills—the human and the divine—into harmony.

Free will stands always between remembrance and forgetting. Remembrance is turning to the One as the upright path. Forgetting abandons the self to its fall toward the lowest levels—earth and darkness, dispersion and chaos. Recalling our original and authentic station and covenant with God, we see ourselves stretched between Peace, our highest possibility, and chaos and darkness in the depths of our passions. The desire for Peace appears as a great war in the self. In it, the self oriented toward Peace tries to overcome the self prone to evil or void. All human wars in the external world are little compared to this war in the self.[8]

7. FAITH

As aspects of human wholeness, fear and will shape our relationship toward what we encounter as otherness. Fear is a response to the unknown. We may flee from the unknown or oppose it. Either course may involve measured or unmeasured response. A measured response involves the will. Human voluntary action is always a choice between possibilities: "I will" or "I will not." Judgment may be shaped by various forms of knowledge on the part of the individual deploying reason in the attempt to survive and be happy. But, as humans, we never have absolute knowledge. Our knowledge is always attained through comparison (analogy) or experiment. But God is not like anything. The highest human knowledge is therefore consciousness of the unknowability of God, even though nothing except Him is real and so nothing other than Him may be known. That is why the prophet prays in response to God's command[1]:

> O God, I seek refuge in Thy pleasure from Thy wrath, and in Thy forgiveness from Thy punishment, and I seek refuge in Thee from Thee.[2]

We always exist in some place and at some time. We may take various directions, but our innermost nature turns us onto the path to the

Watering Hole. If that watering hole is the One, then and then alone can it reveal itself to us as the call and the way. The choice of one out of infinite possibilities is always made out of free will. Although one must admit that only God's will is free, we cannot accept the Debt or our relationship to it under duress: "No compulsion is there regarding the Debt."[3] Everything we have, we have received from God, including our free will as a condition of confidence.[4] Our free will means always facing the choice between "it is" and "it is not." As this is on the basis of limited knowledge, no choice is free of fear. Free will entails choice and so fear. Only when fear focuses on the Unity can one speak of overcoming fear of conditioned or finite things. If the Debt were to be returned under coercion, confidence or the relationship of good faith would lose all sense. This is the authentic relationship between human being and God.[5] God is Faithful, and our covenant with Him is conditioned by our faithfulness.

That God refrains from force in His relationship with humanity as His image permits agreement, covenant, or oath. The relationship is based on free will. We can realize our authentic and beautiful nature in relationship with ourselves, our families and society, and the world as a whole only by shaping our nature after the beautiful divine names. In the interpretation of the Debt given by the Angel Gabriel to the Prophet, the first name used to define Him is the divine name of Peace (*al-Salām*).

Every choice made on the basis of free will involves separation from the apparent and the passing with a view to connection (*religio, din*)[6] with the Highest or God. Realization in authentic creaturehood means bearing witness to Unity and accepting confidence. Having been created in splendid uprightness is the source of our ability to realize the beautiful divine names in the self and so discover our own most beautiful character. Attaining beauty of character is our covenant with God:

> Only men possessed of minds remember; who fulfill God's covenant, and break not the covenant, who join what God has commanded shall be joined, and fear their Lord, and dread the evil reckoning.[7]

Our will leads to the limit of the world in which our reason acts. It does not comprehend our entire being. Will is always touched by love and knowledge. We love what we feel or know as good for us, and what we know and feel as good for us we love. There is no love without knowledge, no knowledge without love. They may not be separated without denial of human wholeness. Love and knowledge together are faith. There is both love and knowledge in every faith, but the relationships between them vary. We come to know what we want and come to love what we know, so long as it is in accord with our innate need to survive and be happy.

We face the world as externality which determines us, while our self and the world as a whole form a pair seeking one and the same cause. The constant flux of both world and human being does not invalidate our love of final cause or final purpose. We want that cause and that purpose and try to come to know them in everything that is in either the external world or ourselves. The greater the love for them, the greater the need to know them. And vice versa, the love for them is greater as knowledge of them grows. He is the reason and the purpose, God, the One. The coupling of love and knowledge is faith in Him.

Given that our knowledge is through binary oppositions—and everything in existence is formed of such oppositions—we recognize the visible quantifiable world as derived from a higher world, which is invisible and unquantifiable. In line with this, and we are called to this by the lesson on the Debt, we learn that the other world is more real than this. We are called to confess and accept the angels as God's heralds and closer to the other world. These heralds are not to be recognized as though they were phenomena in the world of will and reason. They are inseparable from love for the Highest and not to be distinguished from their consequences in the visible and quantifiable world. After they have been recognized, the material world appears a confirmation of a higher or spiritual world. In this way, we find the answer to material exile in our essential and highest right: not to die with the material dissolution.

This interconnectedness of the invisible and visible worlds, in which the angels are envoys and deliverers of news and decisions, leads us to self-knowledge through the possibility of relationship with the Unseen. To make clearer to us what is revealed in the creation of the heavens and the earth, God sent down and revealed the Book. Thus, the revelation of God is present in human language. These books have been sent down and revealed to chosen individuals who are prophets and messengers to humankind. They have been many, and many languages have received the revealed book, but the message is in essence one and the same. The one God has sent many prophets and messengers to us with guidance and books. The reason for doing so is our good and to provide measures that we may judge and be judged for every atom of good done and every atom of evil done. Faith in God's prophets and messengers and the divine Book entails love for them as instances and means of the revelation of God. This love is inseparable from knowledge of the prophets and the books. Faith in angels, books, and messengers is love for them and knowledge of them. In them, we recognize the world in which we stand and our own self as divine revelation and discourse.

Pure human nature involves a tendency to the beautiful and the good, as well as to justice and peace. We are never deprived of these tendencies even at our worst. But neither the beauty nor the good toward which we turn are ever absolute. They are our highest goal. But God alone is absolute Beauty, Goodness, Justice, and Peace.[8]

We are as such the possibility of perfectibility. We realize this possibility in covenant with God, to Whom the beautiful names belong. Wheresoever human being is, covenant with God binds it to turn from the lower to the higher, that character may be shaped by the beautiful names. This turning is an infinite ascent or up-straightening, and the prophets are the most beautiful examples of it.[9] Their characters were shaped by oath to God and reception of His names. They were enlightened, for God is Light; peaceful, for God is Peace; praised, for God is Praised; beautiful, for God is Beautiful; patient, for God is Patient; merciful, for God is Merciful; faithful, for God is Faithful; wise, for God is Wise; and they were so entirely such in their selves as to be His images. When the book was revealed to them, the prophets confirmed it through their characters and were examples to their followers of justice, goodness, and beauty. This is why God ordered the Praiser to say:

> People of the Book, you do not stand on anything, until you perform the Torah and the Gospel, and what was sent down to you from your Lord.[10]

Every prophet is such, but covenant with God entails direct connection with one and recognition of all. To each prophet one may apply what the Praiser says of himself:

> None of you is a believer till I am dearer to him than his child, his father and the whole mankind.[11]

This command is decisive: Accepting it, we reject everything, to receive everything from God.[12] Relationship with things, including our parents and children, is meaningful only insofar as they are signs of God. Everything belongs to God, to Whom there is no other.[13] Not even parents or children have any meaning outside of witness to Unity. To follow the commandment means turning and returning to Unity, revealed through His signs in the world and the self. This is the way to follow the Prophet, whom God commanded to say:

> Say, "If you love God, follow me, and God will love you and forgive you your sins; God is All-forgiving, All-merciful."[14]

Love for God is the desire that everything in the world and the self bear witness to Unity and that Unity bear witness to everything: Everything is from God and everything returns to God,[15] for God is One,[16] and the Prophet is "the most beautiful example,"[17] "of the most sublime character,"[18] "a light-giving lamp,"[19] and the "first of the people-of-peace."[20]

Justice is our highest aspiration. It is, however, attainable only in God Who knows everything and accordingly may judge everything absolutely justly. Therefore, faith in the last day, as the place and time of absolute justice, is the greatest love and the greatest knowledge possible for human being. Through this turn to justice and just judgment, which means putting everything in its proper place, we recognize meaning and the possibility of peace and harmony, both here and after. Peace and harmony are balance and orientation. We have been given the possibility to judge justly and not to fall short in assessment. We are called to such a relationship toward the world and ourselves in the lesson on the Debt taught by the Angel Gabriel, who brought a call and guidance from God. But full measure and full justice will be attained for each thing and every spoken word when everything is weighed on the last day. People may differ in regard to their questions or ideas about higher invisible reality. But there can be no excuse for unjust living or action with regard to other people and things in the world. The final judgment is the supreme measure of love and knowledge. It is also the source of the greatest fear, surpassing all other fears, and of the greatest hope, embracing all others. Just action and judgment with regard to the other are the only measures of our aspiration for harmonization of our will with God's.

We came into the world out of a drop of insignificant liquid. That insignificant drop's love to reveal itself, which is nothing other than the Creator's love for His own self-revelation, shepherds us from our first hour to our death. At death, we cross the boundary, of which we can know nothing except our profound sense that life, which includes both happiness and suffering, must have some meaning. Knowledge of what is after death is not possible, however, except on the basis of the call sent by the Creator through His angels, prophets, and books. According to them, we will rise and account for our earthly life. He, before Whom we will stand and give account, is God, our Creator and Judge.

8. Beauty

Being-at-peace means willing acceptance, including acceptance of being separated from the apparent and passing for the sake of connection with the real and lasting. Being-at-peace is liberation from everything that is not God and subordination to Him alone. Whosoever is obedient to God, who is His servant, becomes His worldly vicegerent. Everything in existence is subordinate to this vicegerent and announces our true position to us. Unity appears as the Principle of all because everything is indebted to Him alone. Only through Unity do the things in existence and existence as a whole enjoy reality. Being-at-peace is therefore simultaneously liberation and service. Only one who is liberated of all dependence, except on the Independent, may participate in the freedom of the Infinite. This is the meaning of our free attempt to ensure that God's will be done on earth as it is in heaven.

Our success in transforming will into love, or orientation toward the Beloved, and then love into knowledge is always manifest in the dichotomy of being and knowledge. Although we can know what we are not, we want to be what we know. Closeness to Him Who knows is proof that we have reduced the gap between being and knowledge. We come to know Him we love and cannot be satisfied with anything less than absolute closeness to Him. At our core is the authentic nature whereby we were created for the Creator. That is why our purpose is unlimited. No situation we may attain is sufficient to the dignity allocated us by God through the Holy Spirit. All the beauty in us and our world has been directly received. It is the recognition of eternity in the finite. And we want it and to be with it.

Beauty is revelation of the good. Only in good can we find and confirm the reason for our existence. Beauty announces God, Who is Beautiful and loves beauty.[1] That annunciation takes place in a countless multitude of places and times. None of them can fully express His beauty even though it may be present anywhere. When we recognize the beauty of our Creator in all the things of the world and feel His gaze in every place and at every hour, our being has come close to our knowing. We gather beauty, sensing its attractiveness, for it is nothing other than manifestation of the Beautiful and the Merciful. We exemplify being-at-peace with the Beautiful. We subordinate ourselves to Him as a loyal servant, with love for Him and the feeling that He is looking over us at every moment. We want to be such that He sees us as His beloved and as beautiful. Talking of the inseparability of the lover who approaches the beloved, God speaks through Muhammad:

> My servant draws near to Me through nothing I love more than that which I have made obligatory to him. My servant never ceases drawing near to Me through supererogatory works until I love him. Then, when I love him, I am his hearing through which he hears, his sight through which he sees, his hand through which he grasps, and his foot through which he walks.[2]

This tradition, in which God speaks through the Prophet Muhammad, is to be found in the collection of *Sahih al-Bukhari*, one of the key texts of the islamic tradition. Our free aspiration, in love and knowledge, to achieve identification with the will of God points toward the ultimate result of confession that there is no god but God and that Muhammad is His servant and His messenger. Declaring divine Unity, we see ourselves in and through the divine signs in the world and the self. These signs receive and radiate praise of the Creator and acknowledge the Praiser as the highest possibility for us as humans. We become a pure image of the Highest, but an image realized under conditions of creaturehood and, therefore, in relationship with others.

This relationship with others involves getting to know the self. The other and the different are always both potentially better and worse than the one in relationship with them. Nothing can be gained or lost in others without potentially causing gain or loss at the same time in oneself. In every choice, which is always "for one" and not "for another," the call is made to set up our own measure as absolute truth. But human being can approach the truth only through that which reveals it. Tensions between them (the truth and that which reveals it) are remoteness from Peace.

Invocation of Peace and salutation in the name of Peace are at the heart of the islamic relationship to other people, regardless of how and why they differ. Peace is one of God's names. Invoking God in relation to other people is the same as directing intercourse through Him as eternal witness. Each one of us is on the path toward the House of Peace. Given that difference exists between us as perfect possibility and the Hour, no human condition can be said to represent arrival at the House. That is the reason Peace is the highest aspiration of every person-of-peace. We attempt to bring our relations with both enemies and friends, near and far, into harmony with this aspiration. One cannot talk of politics or of economics, of the family or of neighborhood, of earth or of heaven without taking on board the primacy of Peace.

So, if we would seek Peace as a precondition to survival and good fortune, we must afford the other the same possibility. Their relations involve connection to Peace as fullness or the one unchanging God. The person-of-peace (*muslim*) is on the path toward being-at-peace (*islam*) which leads through all the particularities of the world and the world as a whole to Peace (*al-Salām*). One must continuously repeat that the relationship of the person-of-peace (*muslim*) and Peace (*al-Salām*) is being-at-peace (*islam*).[3] This person-of-peace/being-at-peace/Peace relationship may be denied and corrupted in various ways. When it ceases to be what the holy texts say of it, however, then either God, who is not determinable, or connections with Him are transformed into determinate phenomena. Something from His creation has been associated to God, than whom there is no other God, whether it is signs in the world or the self or human ideas and passions. Any association to God (idolatry) means service of the limited and unconditional in the place of the unlimited and absolute.[4] Such service denies or limits free will, resulting in injustice and violence. Whenever we claim knowledge of God such that we can determine Him, we have denied that there is no god but God.

Being a person-of-peace on the path toward Peace receives confirmation throughout existence—in the world and all its signs, in the human sense-of-self and its experiences, in the revealed books and the prophets whose witness they are. Wherever we find signs and stimulus for the journey toward Peace, there too is beauty. The revelation in three books—the cosmic, the human, and the prophetic—requires recognition of the possibilities in each of us. Without such recognition the world and the things in it remain meaningless. Everything in existence was created with truth.

The relationship with the other and the different requires distinction of the true from the untrue and cleaving to the true. Thus is human being in continuous discovery of beauty as God's closeness to us. And only through the simultaneous closeness and remoteness of God, suggested by His names of incomparability and similarity, may we recognize and realize ourselves as the end of creation or as descent and the possibility that by gathering in ourselves the totality of existence or all of the divine names we may return to Him as the Near One.

We cannot do this without humility and generosity toward the other and the different. When we are oriented toward and set off for that goal, we follow the Prophet as the Light and the Most Beautiful Example. Wherever we may be, our potential is more than we are at that time. For us to be on the path toward attainment of our highest potential, we need knowledge of what our highest potential is. It is nothing other than the perfect human being, in whom the beautiful divine names are realized, who finds God in everything and returns to Him in peace.

God says to the Prophet, "Thou art of the most sublime character."[5] Character describes a person's manner of life, "innate disposition" or "nature" in the widest sense of that term, as well as "habitual behavior" that becomes, so to speak, "second nature." The Prophet's character, according to the statement of his widow, Aisha, was the Recitation.[6] The Prophet was asked about the most beautiful character. On different occasions, he gave the following answers:

Among the best of you is the most beautiful in character traits.[7]

The most beloved to Me amongst you is one who has the most beautiful character traits.[8]

God will admit into paradise any person-of-peace, whose beautiful character is attested by four persons.[9]

I was sent to perfect beautiful character.[10]

As may be seen from the Prophet's sayings, our highest potential is beauty of character. Such beauty of character is attained through the divine attributes or names. This is because "His beautiful names" define our relationship toward God. In this way, we attain "beauty of character" through the names. Many moral attributes are, in fact, divine attributes. The turner is one who through turning establishes a relationship with God as the Turner; the faithful is one who through faith establishes a relationship with God as the Faithful; and the forgiving is one who through forgiveness establishes a relationship with God as the Forgiving; the clement is one who establishes a relationship through clemency with God as the Clement; the loving, one who through love establishes a relationship with God as the Loving; the just, one who establishes a relationship through justice with God as the Just; the patient, one who establishes a relationship through patience with God as the Patient; the wise, one who establishes a relationship through wisdom with God as the Wise.[11] And so on, through all the beautiful names of God, so that the name of wrath stimulates us to seek sanctuary in God from God, to direct ourselves from the lowest depths toward most beautiful uprightness. One should stress that we relate to God through countless signs in the world and the self. Through those signs or through His words, God reveals Himself to us. The path of spiritual realization is the reception of the divine attributes and names in human character.

Only two things are certain for any of us—the present and death. Both are such that we try to avoid them like the fullness of the real. We turn from the now, where voluntary liberation from the apparent and the passing and cleavage to the real and lasting would be possible, to yesterday and tomorrow. In the immediacy of life in the now, we look for reasons in an infinity of responses to the questions of whence and why we are in this here and now. Preoccupation with these questions turns us from the possibilities offered by the security of the now. We try to plan and determine our tomorrow at the expense of the security of our now.

It is not uncommon for us to flee the security of the now into the insecurity of the past and the future, which are the less secure the more remote we are from ourselves. Although our dignity is primarily connected with the question of the spirit, its affliction and redemption, our existence also requires answers to the question of the dignity of our bodies and our or its relationship with other people, both near and far, both friends and enemies. Whatever answer is reached, it will remain incomplete as long as human being is not always an eye with which God sees, an ear with which God hears, or a sense-of-self which is pure image of the Sense-of-self. That is a level of being in which the beauty and love of the Creator are clearly apparent in all the signs in the world and in ourselves. The beauty we see in the signs throughout existence attracts the seer and what attracts us is what we know. Attraction may only be ended by becoming what is known and knowing what is wanted.

9. THE HOUR

Every self experiences the external world as an indisputable and clear reality. Insecurity in the self takes that externality for its object and expresses itself as the experience of mundane imperfection. The self undertakes to change the external world, seeking *liberation* from its imperfections and wildness. Attempts to change the world most commonly take place without any questioning of the subject which *knows* it and intends to *fix* it. This whole relationship to the external world, as incomplete, while taking the self to be complete, is flight from the Hour, which is the Real, and a search for security outside of the Hour and outside the self which the Hour never abandons.

Forgetting the decisiveness of the Hour and finding reasons to deny it produce distortion of the train from higher to lower, placing the body above the self and family and society above the individual. In this forgetting, the One is ignored or denied as the principle of multiplicity. Through inversion, the sublime righteousness in which human being was originally created becomes lowliness and orientation toward this world instead of that, toward the lower instead of the higher, toward the material instead of the spiritual. Under such circumstances, the servant gives birth to the mistress and the self is raised above the Spirit, human being above God, earth above Heaven, and so forth.

Then, we pretend to be free, no longer accepting that we are entirely dependent servants of our Creator, beyond even our original unshod and naked shepherdhood. We take ourselves for master and our doings for more than all the rest of creation. We cease to be servant to the King, whose vicegerent on earth we are. We assume sovereignty over all existence. But our being barefoot, explicitly alluded to in the tradition of the meeting of the Angel Gabriel and the Prophet the Praised, signifies our nature, our inseparability from earth.

Whatever form our separation may take, it is artificial; our barefootedness is essential. So is our nakedness. We are entirely naked before the Truth and can hide nothing. This returns us to our nature as shepherd, where everything we have or may have has been given and entrusted for safekeeping. Entrusted with everything we have for safekeeping, we are obliged to justice. Everything that has been given to us bears the dignity of the Giver, and safekeeping is the only way to protect our own dignity. To begin with, we owe no debt to anyone except God. Our relationship to God is through all the signs in the inner and outer worlds, signs that are not God but have no reality aside from Him.

If we deny the truth of having received everything we have, we put our original dignity below the level of our changing condition. Then, we may learn only through other things. We know no fullness, from which everything arrives in existence and to which it returns, nor any eternal measure, according to which things may be known. Then there is nothing which might determine our responsibility.

When we lose sight of our original nature, when we forget that there is no god but God, then our whole interpretation of the world becomes inverted, the derived becomes the principle, the principle derived, the central peripheral, the peripheral central. Then the world appears to us evil and ugly, and we try to subordinate and render it good and beautiful, recognizing no goodness or beauty beyond our own position at the pinnacle of development from darkness and undifferentiated primal fog. Thus, created beings who have taken themselves for the acme of development make of themselves a god or make their god in their own image, a work of their imagination.

The debt of which the Angel Gabriel teaches, transferring knowledge from God, requires a completely other course: We are obliged only to our Creator and our self-realization in our original nature is consciousness of that debt and acceptance of the obligation it involves. To demonstrate our relationship to the Hour, the Prophet Muhammad once said, "I and the Hour are like this!"[1] displaying his index and middle fingers joined together. In this way, he, the most beautiful example chosen by God, showed that he had realized himself within the Hour and, as the most beautiful example, represented the potential of the real in every human being, while remaining close all his life to those around him, especially the humble and dejected, the persecuted and the oppressed. All his life, he too experienced humility and rejection, persecution and oppression. It is difficult to imagine any human affliction through which he did not pass.

Accepting that God is the always and everywhere present Other and that, consequently, the entirely different—the dejected and the poor, the foreign and the sick, the unknown and the unreasonable— are part of the human condition, the Praised considered life with the poor, the humble, the sick, and the persecuted a way of bearing witness to the covenant with God. That covenant is a contract in which God as Peace entrusts to the person-of-peace sublime capacity—being the Praised, the Most Beautiful Example, the Light-Bearing Lamp, the Most Sublime Character.

The two adjacent and inseparable fingers in the Prophet's discourse represent the Hour and the Prophet himself as the most beautiful example. His discourse was directed toward his listeners. To each, it was said: The hour you are in is your reality, and flight from that hour is delusion. You may realize your sublime potential in yourselves in this Hour, but flight into yesterday or tomorrow is nothing but turning from God as the Real toward the unreal; if you accept the reality of the Hour and find in it your authentic nature, then you follow me because you love God and realize within yourselves God's love toward you. That is human realization in mercy, which surpasses divine wrath. It is our flowing into or return to God.

Consciousness of the Hour is inseparable from justice and fairness. Human responsibility for justice may not be deferred and consciousness of the Hour as fully imminent is prompted by all those deprived of justice. So, in the *Sahih Muslim*, a further collection of traditions, it is recorded of the Prophet Muhammad that God speaks through him:

Verily, God, the Exalted and Glorious, would say on the Day of Resurrection, "O son of Adam, I was sick but you did not visit me." He would say, "O my Lord; how could I visit Thee whereas Thou art the Lord of the worlds?" Thereupon He would say, "Didn't you know that such and such servant of mine was sick but you did not visit him and were you not aware of this that if you had visited him, you would have found Me by him? O son of Adam, I asked food from you but you did not feed me." He would say, "My Lord, how could I feed thee whereas Thou art the Lord of worlds?" He said, "Didn't you know that such and such servant of mine asked food from you but you did not feed him, and were you not aware that if you had fed him you would find him by My side? O son of Adam, I asked drink from you but you did not provide Me." He would say, "My Lord, how could I provide Thee whereas Thou art the Lord of worlds?" Thereupon He would say, "Such and such servant of mine asked you for drink but you did not provide him, and had you provided him drink you would have found him near Me."[2]

Although the Hour is normally interpreted as the threat of final and absolute judgment and the resolution of all injustice in the future world, it cannot be separated from the possibilities each human individual has now. It is the acceptance of God's closeness and the primacy of His mercy. What cannot be avoided on the day of Resurrection or in the final reckoning is also required here and now as our responsibility to God, before Whose face every self finds itself, always and everywhere. Responsibility before the Face, Which reveals Himself through His signs in all the worlds, entails responsibility in the face of everything that is in the visible universe.

Our responsibility to the external world as a whole and to all the particularities within it is at the same time responsibility to ourselves, as there is nothing in the world or the self that does not reveal the Truth. The whole world praises God:[3]

> The seven heavens and the earth, and whosoever in them is, extol Him; nothing is, that does not proclaim His praise, but you do not understand their extolling.[4]

This celebration of praise is the world's covenant with God. God is All-praised,[5] and He reveals His praisedness in His creation. The relationship between everything created as a revelation of God's praise and God as the Creator is praise. Everything that exists is a praising thing connected to God as All-praised through praise. The ability of the worlds to praise God is their tranquility in His Peace, as He says, "And they have found peace in Him whoso is in the heavens and the earth."[6]

Given that human being is the sum of all creation in the worlds and that we bring together in our selves earthly corporeality and divine Spirit, we, too, are in covenant with God. Our highest capacity is to realize our character as sublime righteousness, from which we began and to which we can return out of the depths of the lowest earthly station. The Praised is the best model for that return and the perfect guide. He is the example of the full covenant of the worlds and realized humanity, the two images of praising one and the same God as the All-praised. In this return, we are always in the Hour, which never abandons us and whose imminence is like God's. We cannot flee the Hour, and so acceptance of its closeness is the same as acceptance of God's. God says, "I am near"[7] and "We are nearer to him than the jugular vein."[8] The indubitable and inevitable imminence of the Hour as the truth of God is contained in God's message, "Son of Adam, abuse not the time, whereas I am the time since in My hands are the day and the night."[9] Related to this is God's statement:

> To God belongs the Unseen in the heavens and in the earth. And the matter of the Hour is as a twinkling of the eye, or nearer. Surely God is powerful over everything.[10]

The evident imminence of the Hour, from which we impotently try to escape into forgetfulness and show, and the apparent remoteness of death that we have no wish to see as real imminence are key elements of the Debt and of any lesson on it. Both the Hour and Death are nigh, for God, as the Creator of everything, is the Giver of Life and Death, infinitely close to everything in existence. Therefore the lesson of the two sure things—the Hour and Death—is supplemented by two more—resurrection and judgment. Nor can one read the Recitation without recognizing that what God says about the Hour and Death is inseparable from what is said about the Day of Resurrection and the Day of Judgment.

The surety of the Hour, from which we flee into yesterday and tomorrow, is, according to the Recitation, equivalent to the surety of the resurrection of the dead and the judgment of every self. In this surety, finitude will be transformed from mediacy to immediacy. Because all our relations to signs in the world and the self derive their meaning from witness to divine Unity and links to them are through God, the Ever-present Witness, according to the Recitation, on the Day of Debt, when everything will be measured and accounted for in direct relation to God and without mediation, all other relationships will be broken. Confession that there is no self except the Self will be realized that day. Every self will find itself face to Face with the Self:

> And beware a day when no soul for another shall give satisfaction, and no counterpoise shall be accepted from it, nor any intercession shall be profitable to it, neither shall they be helped.[11]

> Upon that day men shall issue in scatterings to see their works, and whoso has done an atom's weight of good shall see it and whoso has done an atom's weight of evil shall see it.[12]

On that day, all people will be gathered,[13] and the differences between them, attributable to their belonging to their times and peoples, tongues and customs, traditions of learning and ritual, will be measured against the value of good deeds, and no excuse for falling short will be accepted.[14] Every thing will show itself as of original right, and its truth will be revealed accordingly to the prayer of the Prophet, "God, show us things as they are."[15]

10. Humanity

All humanity was created of a single self or a single spirit in accordance with the Debt, as encapsulated in the tale of the meeting and conversation between the Angel Gabriel and the Prophet Muhammad.[1] The meaning of that creation was God's love and desire to be known. God's love revealed in creation has two important aspects in human being. The first is service, the second our station (as vicegerent) on earth. By realizing our nature as servant, we open ourselves to receive the attributes of our Creator. Taking on such attributes and displaying our nature as recipient, we are enabled for action in the world, which is entrusted to us as part of our totality and orientation toward our higher potential.

Being human means feeling the debt toward oneself, to others, and to the world. Every connection between one human being and another is, in fact, a debt: There is always something we have received and something we have given. Sometimes we are in debt, sometimes the debt is to us. Through witness to God's Unity, we confess that everything in the world or self derives its reality from God. Everything owes a debt to God, as there is no real outside the Real. The world, as the revelation of God, has a certain received reality so that connection with anything is connection with God. If, however, it is denied in such connection that every debt belongs to God alone, witness to Unity is covered or denied. Debt in its ultimate sense belongs only to God but is realized with regard to the world and all its phenomena.

All of humanity stems from one human self or spirit. People are divided into various tribes, peoples, races, and languages and are settled in different parts of the world in order that they may know and compete with each other in good.[2] None of these variations evade God. They are His revelation, for each particular needs everything that is in the world to come to know God, which is the same as coming to know oneself. By coming to know each other and competing in good, people learn the reason and purpose of their creation. The Unity from which they are arisen is nothing other than the most beautiful righteousness or His image. Coming to know His image, they come to know Him. Given that we are here talking of Him as eternity and infinity, His revelation takes place only through unlimited flow and exchange. Every particular in the totality of creation has something to say about this. To deny that means not to accept that everything has been created in truth.

Given that human being is open to this totality, listening and speaking are also an infinite stream through which God reveals Himself. Accordingly, no human being can be surplus or pointless to this revelation. Our nature as a being related to our Creator through confidence allows us to set ourselves up and act with the greatest possible closeness to non-being, which is equivalent to the greatest remoteness from God although this remoteness is ours alone and not God's. For God is always and everywhere nigh.[3] Only human being may be remote.

Through division into tribes, peoples, races, and languages, people have become a multitude in which divine Unity appears. To all of them God is Creator, Guardian, and Judge. His creation is His discourse. To learn of His creation means to learn of Him. His creation has never been bereft of His mercy. It is left up to people to be in confidence with Him and to relate to Him on the basis of free will, but He does not abandon them.[4]

God comprehends everything in His Knowledge and His Mercy.[5] He is the final judge of everything we do, which means that of His free will He has enabled us to act according to free will. In His Knowledge and His Will, God has allowed us to experience and display our full potential. But He never leaves us at that. He is always with us and before us. He sees and hears us. He is with us wherever we are. He is closer to us than our jugular vein,[6] and He answers to our call.[7]

His reply is also His sending of the prophets and the books to show men the way to Himself. There have always and everywhere been such prophets and books. There has been no people to whom He has not sent His guides.[8] They have revealed His unity, just as the sky and the earth do: different prophets to different peoples in different tongues: one Creator of many worlds and many prophets of one Creator.

Many prophets at different times have declared His unity. These declarations have taken on historical form in Judaism, Buddhism, Confucianism, Christianity, Islam, and so on. One may speak of them as traditions and civilizations which have endured. Even today, they play a decisive role in our presence on earth and his quest for answers to fatal questions. But everywhere on earth, in human memory and in the remains left by human presence, one can point to traditions and civilizations that have disappeared.

Looking at the stream of the extinction of traditions and civilizations, one may say from the point-of-view of the Debt that the main causes are human forgetting of the origin and end and betrayal of the call to be just. That call, present in every holy tradition, presupposes and includes our ability to distinguish truth from lie, good from evil, beauty from ugliness. This is failure not merely to distinguish them in the general flow but also to cleave to truth, good, and beauty. Such adherence, evident in witness to God and His prophet, may be confirmed only through righteousness. All witness without righteousness is false. Through adherence, we realize ourselves in the world and the world in us. In this process of realization, the other plays a decisive role: through the other, we may determine our own limits and come to know that they are only one of an infinite number of ways of showing the Absolute, as God is on whichever side we care to turn to.[9]

Our presence in the stream and flux of all that is may be viewed in two ways. First, we may be considered to participate in that infinite stream starting at point A and ending at point B. Our position is then a reflection of the total stream before that point and as individuals we cannot significantly influence its course into the future. The other way of interpreting the stream is to take us as individuals open toward eternity and infinity, fully capable of happiness and redemption.

Traditional doctrine teaches that each human being simultaneously is in and transcends history. On the horizontal axis, we are present in space and time, but on the vertical, we are turned toward God. Each human being is in principle a child of the Hour and of one and the same Father. We are not and cannot be mere drops imprisoned in the unknown stream of time between indeterminable antiquity and incomprehensible future. We contain the possibility of transcending remoteness from God, approaching Him, and so coming to know ourselves in His great purpose.

Human freedom, which is just service to absolute truth, absolute good, and absolute beauty, is not and cannot be determined by historical circumstances. Each individual is capable of freedom, but it cannot be realized on the basis of merely rational capacities. Excessive reliance on instrumental reason can result in a break with tradition. Tradition includes, but cannot be reduced to, instrumental reason. Tradition essentially means openness of the lower toward the higher through the levels of Being up to the Absolute. Instrumental Reason can lead us only to the boundary of the limited or finite world. If the boundary is accepted as marking the end or closure of Being, human being is also closed and in this way human perfectibility limited. In Tradition, in the full sense of the word, no limits are set to our perfectibility, because God is Peace, and Peace is from Him. From the traditional point-of-view, openness and perfectibility are manifest in each thing as signs on the path toward the Absolute. Traveling along this path means focusing on the sign only for the sake of the everywhere present Signified to which it points. In other words, mystery is present in everything that exists, as a sign of that which transcends it. Accordingly, we can say that signs always give us very limited knowledge, which does, however, orient or lead us toward the Absolute. Through this limited knowledge, which is not our aim, even though we can know little of Him Who is revealed through these signs, we can come to love Him fully and without limitation. Knowledge and love fused in the totality of human being are belief.

The famous "disenchantment of the world" is the exclusion of love for the sake of knowledge, the absolutization of knowledge. In this way, instrumental reason can attain full knowledge only within the limited or finite world. Reason is just one level of existence, while tradition recognizes and accepts our ability to find Unity in everything, from first to last, from inner to outer. For God is inner and outer. When He is in, the outside is unreal and inverted as there is no god but God. Nor does dialogue cease at any boundary between the various levels of existence. Prophecy is proof of the connection between the various levels of Being.

If human being is reduced to instrumental reason as our highest capacity, then we limit ourselves and our world to what is visible and quantifiable. The world is always more than that, however. The visible and measurable are just a revelation of a higher something that is neither visible nor measurable:

> Have they not regarded what lies before them and what lies behind them of heaven and earth?[10]

Instrumental reason leads to the limit of the quantifiable world, but not past it. Intellect transcends it. Just as Reason reveals multiplicity at a given level of existence but Intellect allows all boundaries to be transcended, so intercourse (or dialogue) facilitates relations between individualities, but discourse assigns them meaning within creation as a whole. The relationship between Intellect and Discourse is manifest in the prophets. They delimit levels of existence. Their intercourse with people of different times and languages allows them to reveal themselves in their authentic uprightness, which is distributed across all the levels of existence. This possibility makes every individual equivalent in worth to all people together:

Therefore we prescribed for the Children of Israel that whoso slays a soul not to retaliate for a soul slain, nor for corruption done in the land, shall be as if he had slain mankind altogether; and whoso gives life to a soul, shall be as if he had given life to mankind altogether.[11]

Your creation and your upraising are but as a single soul. God is All-hearing, All-seeing.[12]

Humanity is in principle a single community. Its existence in time entails development through tradition over generations, but also constant connection with the One, to Which it is sometimes near, sometimes remote. Distancing from or approaching that Unity is an element of overall development:

The people were one nation; then God sent forth the Prophets, good tidings to bear and warning, and He sent down with them the Book with the truth, that He might decide between the people touching their differences; and only those who had been given it were at variance upon it, after the clear signs had come to them, being insolent one to another; then God guided those who believed to the truth, touching which they were at variance, by His leave.[13]

Humanity sprang from one father and one mother, as a primordial community. But it has appeared in history as multiplicity and difference. So it is a community of communities, each of which affords its members a primordial openness toward the ever-present Unity:

Every nation has its Messenger; then when their Messenger comes, justly the issue is decided between them, and they are not wronged.[14]

That fundamental openness of every community toward revelation enables the distinction of truth and lie, which is the precondition for just judgment of the responsibility of individuals and the community: "All have degrees according to what they have done."[15]

Each individual is created in most beautiful uprightness as an image of God. As such, we relate to our Creator as foundation and goal. Every state involves simultaneous closeness to God and distance from Him. We are always between descent and return. This "in-betweenness" is determined by our having been formed of earth and, as regards our inner self, the breathing in of the divine Spirit. But human being is also always externality, shaped by the outer world as a whole. The microcosm of body and spirit corresponds to the macrocosm of earth and heaven.

Every individual is situated in time and space, in a people and a language. Our being "in between" and traveling toward the Goal take place within these conditions, but do not end with them. That all people return to God means that the Goal gathers and connects diversity. The Goal does not destroy difference. It renders it distinct and intelligible. In the end, these differences appear as human realization in relationship with God, as fundamental self-realization through attainment of the Goal. Learning to know others and competing with them in doing good is to discover and confess the divine attributes in one's being, to realize authentic perfection at one's core and to return. That is realization of the most beautiful divine names in one's own nature, in accordance with the saying of the Prophet, "Among the best of you is the most beautiful in character traits."[16]

11. THE OTHER AND THE DIFFERENT

Humanity is an authentic whole. Its division into tribes, peoples, and races does not abrogate the original perfection of each individual or the possibility of our redemption in perfection. Each of us must present our own account and is responsible for every atom of good or evil done. Humanity as such is shaped by its innermost nature or consciousness of the Creator's Unity. All of creation is an expression or utterance of the Creator. So is human being. Human speech, in its purity, is an expression of authentic human nature. That is the essence of all languages, whatever the differences between them. Regardless of the point-of-view or the identity a human being speaks from, regardless of what we find peace in, all individuals and all human communities stand before one and the same God. Our Books either directly or indirectly determine us, as criteria and guidance:

> Dispute not with the People of the Book save in the fairer manner, except for those of them that do wrong; and say, "We believe in what has been sent down to you; our God and your God is One, and in Him we have found peace."[1]

The sending down of the revelation to the prophet and its transmission to people are what shape the peoples of the Book. The Book as we know it is only the materialized form of the Revelation. God sent down His Revelation to the heart, mind, and tongue of the prophet. He heard and received it as connection with God. Through the Revelation the heights of human potential have been revealed and realized—the nature of which renders known the most beautiful divine names. From that which is heard, received, and adopted comes the annunciation to others, always in a language and form of life intelligible to them.

The Book as inscription or reading of what is received and spoken becomes a link with the prophet and God. Whenever that link is ignored or lost, the Book and the doctrine related to it can become closed within the quantifiable world. But it was intended to expound the way and the journey toward God as our highest possibility. The Book consists of a number of *sura* or separate but linked images, just as the whole of existence comprises a multitude of linked and separate worlds, as does the human sense-of-self.

The received Book (or collection of books) becomes the property of a nation handed down from one generation to the next. Each individual of a people of the Book relates to the Book on the basis of his or her own will. Sense-of-self may be shaped by the history and circumstances of that society, but we realize ourselves through conscious and voluntary response to the call of three books—the external world, our sense-of-self, and the message revealed by God through His prophets. Those who respond to the call are the people within the people, the community within the community. They are the jews amongst the Jews, the christians amongst the Christians, the muslims amongst the Muslims. None of these identifications is unconditional. They are confirmed by adherence to the doctrine, ritual, and virtue through which human being realizes itself in relationship with the Real. In any people or community, only some are such.

> Yet they are not all alike; some of the People of the Book are a
> nation upstanding, that recite God's signs in the watches of the
> night, bowing themselves, believing in God and in the Last Day,
> bidding to honour and forbidding dishonour, vying one with the

other in good works; those are of the righteous. And whatsoever good you do, you shall not be denied the just reward of it.[2]

Divine Unity underlies all human variety and free will, amongst whose consequences is difference:

Mankind were only one nation, then they fell into variance. But for a word that preceded from thy Lord, it had been decided between them already touching their differences.[3]

This difference, whose cause and resolution are the Word, is manifest in the multitude of peoples and languages, as in the multitude of prophets and leaders:

Every nation has its Messenger; then, when their Messenger comes, justly the issue is decided between them, and they are not wronged.[4]

We have sent no Messenger, save with the tongue of his people, that he might make all clear to them.[5]

And We sent never a Messenger before thee except that We revealed to him, saying, "There is no god but I; so serve Me."[6]

Accordingly, the one God reveals His guidance to various nations in various languages. The guidance is given not only in various languages but also in various forms of doctrine, ritual, and virtue.

We have appointed for every nation a holy rite, that they may mention God's name.[7]

And We have sent down to thee the Book with the truth, confirming the Book that was before it, and assuring it. So judge between them according to what God has sent down, and do not follow their caprices, to forsake the truth that has come to thee. To every one of you We have appointed a right way and an open road. If God had willed, He would have made you one nation; but that He may try you in what has come to you. So be you forward in good works; unto God shall you return, all together; and He will tell you of that whereon you were at variance.[8]

Variety of languages, paths, ways, and the difference between them shape the multitude of human communities. None of these differences denies, however, the common essence of humanity. Every individual's connection to God, whether voluntary or constrained, comes to being in a community shaped by, amongst other factors, the Book. These communities have various names—including Judaism, Christianity, and Islam.[9] The essence of them all is faith in God and our full accountability to Him for both good and evil. As a result, faith in God and justice are our redemption, regardless of which of the various doctrines, rites, or traditions of virtue we belong to. This is transformation of the two certainties, the now and death, which may be experienced as visible, into two which are invisible and require faith, God and the Day of Judgment. Although God is invisible, nothing would be visible without Him. The Day of Judgment is similar, as no justice would be attainable without connection to it.

This faith in God and the Last Day cannot be separated from the upright path, the way that is open to the members of the various communities. Both human being and the process of self-realization commemorate and glorify God. The more complete our opening, the more complete the glorification. This open way has various paths on which people build places for the commemoration of God, so that our competition in doing good might be clearly expressed in our different tongues:

> Had God not driven back the people, some by the means of others, there had been destroyed cloisters and churches, oratories and mosques, wherein God's name is much mentioned.[10]

In the various traditions of doctrine, ritual, and virtue, the heart of which is the commemoration of God's names, it is faith in God and Judgment Day and the doing of good works which redeem, while doctrine and ritual are paths on the way to realizing that. There is one word common to all the various religious identities—Jewish, Christian, or Muslim—namely, redemption through and in the one God:

> Say, "People of the Book! Come now to a word common between us and you, that we serve none but God, and that we associate not aught with Him, and do not some of us take others as Lords, apart from God."[11]

Each of us experiences the call as our own. We relate to others through the question, "What is wrong in me and with me?" This question is crucial to acceptance that nothing must be associated to God because God alone is good. We have no right to return evil for anything that comes from outside or from the other. Should we assume such a right, we assign primary value to evil, blame to the other, and infallibility to ourselves. That is the meaning of God's word:

> Not equal are the good deed and the evil deed. Repel with that which is fairer and behold, he between whom and thee there is enmity shall be as if he were a loyal friend.[12]

The highest degree of doing good, which is to say being pure, is attained by the prophets, the just, the martyrs, and the good:

> Whosoever obeys God, and the Messenger—they are with those whom God has blessed, Prophets, just men, martyrs, the righteous; good companions they![13]

The prophets were sent to their peoples at different times, to warn them in their own tongues of the connections between the real and the unreal and how to cleave to the real. Although, like every moment, they were all unique and inimitable, the essence of their discourse was one and the same. That is why the Prophet, the Praised, calls the other prophets—Adam, Noah, Abraham, Moses, Solomon, Jesus, and all 124,000—his brothers,[14] and says their debt to God is one and the same.[15] They are the incarnation of the covenant with God—both that which binds all the worlds and that which appears in human being.

Whenever the nature of any of the prophets is looked into, it proves to be always the same, while the differences between them are simply another form of revelation. God says that He sent prophets to each people.[16] The prophets always spoke in the tongue of the people to which they were sent.[17] His justice allows everyone, regardless of place, time, or language, to return to Him as Peace. That at this time, certain of the revealed books are known, accepted, and preserved— the Torah, the Psalms, the Gospels, and the *Qur'an*, for example—and that they are in particular languages (Hebrew, Aramaic, and Arabic) does not mean that these linguistic communities have an advantage over the others. The contrary, in fact. It means only greater responsibility. Any language may receive the content of the Books, both because they preserve the truth that God sent his guides to every people to speak to them in their own tongue and because difference is translatable only in God. No people should abandon the treasure house of its language to accept what was originally sent down in another. Moreover, Revelation in another language may be accepted only if it becomes part of the linguistic treasure house of the language that receives it.

This may be shown through the examples of Adam, Noah, Abraham, Moses, Jesus, and Muhammad. Like God's other prophets, they were all His servants,[18] which means humble and open to the shaping of their character to God's attributes. Their followers may do the same by being God's servants, not theirs.[19] It is easily proven that the prophets are different expressions of the same human covenant with God and that the Praised, who also appears as the Praiser, represents their innermost nature. In each prophet, God's beautiful names are gathered, and the sublime potential of their characters are realized. In this perfect and harmonious collection of God's names, some of them shape how they will be revealed to other people, which is always a reflection of their covenant with God.

From the moment of his creation, Adam was a realized whole. His original character revealed the beautiful names of God. Through forgetting and transgression of the covenant with God regarding the forbidden tree, this wholeness was darkened. The possibility of regaining it is expressed through the names the Turner[20] and the Receiver of turning.[21] God requires sincerity in turning (repentance) of the faithful.[22] After violating the covenant, Adam turned again to God, opening up the possibility of attaining his original wholeness and returning to his initial station.[23]

Noah had recourse to God as the Wise, Who as such is the Most Just Judge,[24] and he received into himself wisdom and justice as his connection with God. He was therefore both wise and just. Thus, he opposed the stubbornness of the people in denying Unity. Abraham was clement,[25] as his connection to God as Clement was clemency.[26] Moses revealed his self-realization as a human being with God as Patient[27] through patience and being patient.[28] Thus he denies any authority other than God, to be guided by Him alone. Jesus realized his covenant with God through anointment, and thus is the Anointed (Messiah): "The anointment of God" and "Who is there that anoints fairer than God?"[29] Muhammad, as his name itself indicates, marked his self-realization through the names of God by relation to God as the All-praised.[30] So, receiving praise from the All-praised, he relates to Him through praise of Him.

12. Intolerance I

The presentation of the Debt given here, as our being indebted for our existence to God the Creator of everything, has two levels. The first is being-at-peace, the second faith. The first belongs to the sphere of will but is not exhausted by it. Each of the proofs of being-at-peace—witness, prayer, purificatory alms, fasting, and circumambulation of the House—must be carried out on the basis of voluntary decision. Faith transcends will, however. It has no decisive proofs. It is open to human freedom. Even when turned toward certainty, faith is always confirmed by free will. It is split between love, which never appears in any relation to constraint, and knowledge, which also reveals itself as beyond imposition. Being-at-peace and faith are manifest in the prophets, messengers, and the good, who are examples of realization based on the presence of those virtues.[1]

God's prophets realize perfection in accordance with the beautiful names of God. They are examples to others in the endeavor to discover and realize authentic nature because God taught Adam all names.[2] One may say of every prophet that he is a person-of-peace, related to God as Peace through being-at-peace; that he is a person-of-faith, related to God as Faithful through faith; that he is a person of goodness and beauty, related to God as the Good and Beautiful through goodness and beauty. The prophets gather in themselves the beautiful names of God and realize their character according to them. When a prophet is recognized on the basis of one of these names, it is evidence, beyond primordial equality, of a truly unique self.

Human finitude, or the fact that our sense-of-self is determined by being posited between void and Peace, requires a guide who talks one's own language, walks the same streets, and eats the same food.[3] To find our orientation toward Peace, we follow a prophet whose name we know and for whom we find reasons in ourselves, in our language, and in our environment. This prophet becomes our model, our guiding light, the sublime character we wish to adopt. We cannot love anyone like our guide to being-at-peace. We recognize him by the series of divine attributes that mark his human character. But we are concerned by the enigma of the crowd of prophets and their sufferings, as well as by their having been chosen above all others.

We need one guide or model, but we learn of the love others have for other prophets. The crowd of prophets other than ours appears to deny the meaning of their love, as love seeks union, which is possible only with one. This is why many of the seekers of Peace fail to recognize their prophet as just a gate to the One. They take him for a goal, limiting God by their vision of human perfection. That we can fail to recognize the path to God in our prophet is the reason we can fail to accept, and consequently deny or insult, other prophets.

It is possible to find statements in the Recitation which, under the prevailing interpretation, may be considered justificatory warrant for intolerance of the other or different. Although it is clear that the legacy of the prophets is to be found in every people, their wisdom is denied by differentiating between prophets. Adhering to a particular prophet and his legacy and supposing that they have therein everything they need to discover authentic perfection, many people suppose that those outside the boundaries of their individual and collective identities are bereft of wisdom or connection to God. This denies God's lordship of the worlds. For it is clear that other peoples are also connected by their languages and meanings to God. In this way, one falls into the riddle of "the two gods": "God says, 'Take not to you two gods. He is only One God; so have awe of Me!'"[4]

God's call highlights the possibility that men may posit two gods. When this happens, for some, "our god" is right, which necessarily means that "their god" is wrong. Under such circumstances, the people with the "right god" feel better able to realize their goals without or despite the other. If they represent any sort of hindrance to the goal, violence against them is sanctioned. Moreover, it is done in the name of "our god." Such a situation is a denial of Unity and is association unto God. It leads to violence against existence as a whole, which reveals the one and only God.

Such views are diametrically opposed to those presented earlier as examples of tolerance founded on first principles. The reader and interpreter of the Text faces the problem of resolving these contradictions. Failure to resolve it is the predominant source of the condemnation of muslims and the accusation that they lack moral foundation with regard to the other and the different. Such condemnation of muslims is to be found in Christian, Jewish, Hindu, and other approaches to the other who does not belong to the given unit of identification.

We will now present some of the more emphatic statements interpreted as justifying intolerance.

> O believers, take not Jews and Christians as friends; they are friends of each other. Whoso of you makes them his friends is one of them. God guides not the people of the evildoers.[5]

No more than being a Muslim, does being a Jew or a Christian necessarily entail having a particular ethical disposition, equally valid for every member of the group. That these communities are shaped by the Debt or connection to God is clear from the existence of holy people and holy art in each of them. In spite of all their differences, these communities are formed by the Books sent down to them by God and by the beautiful examples of those who brought those Books. These are the communities or peoples whose heritage is of most value in all existence. Simply being a member of one of these communities, however, does not exempt one from the obligation of justice and righteousness, nor exclude the possibility that one may betray it.

This divine call is sent to those who would establish their relations with people on the basis of accountability to the Caller. If they respond to the call, then their relationship with others is with equals in principle before God and not absent ethical rules, regardless of whether they are their fathers or their sons, Jews, Christians, or Muslims. Such affiliation does not release any human being from dependence on God, nor from responsibility:

> And they say, "None shall enter Paradise except that they be Jews or Christians." Such are their fancies. Say, "Produce your proof, if you speak truly."[6]

Belonging to one of the peoples of the Book does not mean every member submits to the process of change in accordance with its teaching. The individual may approach the Book only through his or her own sense-of-self. The purpose of the Book is that the self be changed in line with it. The potential for change is, however, infinite, which is why every interpretation is finite. This means being on a path which cannot be denied to others.

The Book was announced by the absolute Self to the conditioned or finite one. It mediates between the Self which announces it and the self which studies it. On its own, it does not and cannot act as a goal in the place of the Self. The Book published by the Self bit by bit must be read in the same way—bit by bit, even though it exists as a complete inscription preserved in a scroll, a codex, or memory. Every part of it is in conversation with all the rest. Separating a part and using it without the rest may allow a given condition of the conditioned self to be justified. It is, however, denial and alteration of the Book. The Book may be adopted, but without affecting the self. The Book is the inscription of God's discourse, which is inexhaustible. Every interpretation is overflow of that inexhaustibility or demonstration of the superabundance and all-mercy of God. No interpretation may claim finality, nor any sense-of-self completion, as long as it is related to the Book:

> The likeness of those who have been loaded with the Torah then they have not carried it, is as the likeness of an ass carrying books. Evil is the likeness of the people who have cried lies to God's signs. God guides never the people of the evildoers.[7]

> Say, "People of the Book, you do not stand on anything, until you perform the Torah and the Gospel, and what was sent down to you from your Lord."[8]

Every self is conditioned, and its knowledge depends on the Self. Whenever a self takes its condition as the measure of its relations to external phenomena, it shapes the picture according to its condition. In this way, it refuses the command to be *muslim*—humble, calm, modest, obedient, clement, and so forth. When the conditioned "I" is taken as measure, it shapes the Book it studies to itself, and not itself to the Book. It neither takes the Book up nor applies it nor admits the evidence in it of God's superabundance and mercy:

> Are you then so eager that they should believe you, seeing there is a party of them that heard God's word, and then tampered with it, and that after they had comprehended it, wittingly?[9]

> Some of the Jews pervert words from their meanings saying, "We have heard and we disobey" and "Hear, and be thou not given to hear" and "Observe us," twisting with their tongues and traducing the Debt. If they had said, "We have heard and obey" and "Hear" and "Regard us," it would have been better for them, and more upright; but God has cursed them for their covering, so they believe not, except a few.[10]

> Thou wilt surely find the most hostile of men to the believers are the Jews and the idolaters; and thou wilt surely find the nearest of them in love to the believers are those who say, "We are Christians"; that, because some of them are priests and monks, and they wax not proud.[11]

No; Abraham in truth was not a Jew, neither a Christian; but he was a person-of-peace and one pure of faith; certainly he was never of the idolaters. Surely the people standing closest to Abraham are those who followed him, and this Prophet, and those who believe; and God is the Protector of the believers.[12]

These examples allow one to state that in the Recitation God explained the procedure for differentiating the habitual behavior of a certain group—Jews, Christians, Sabaeans, and Magians,[13] for example—and adherence to righteousness, which is not and never can be restricted to any of these groups, nor denied them. Individuals have moral grounds. Societies and communities are merely stages on which their members present their discovery or covering over of those grounds. One can be a person-of-peace while also being a Jew, Christian, or Muslim, and one may equally fail to be. God's command to human being is that he be a person-of-peace, independent of his other affiliations. Accordingly, friendship, as a relationship between individuals, is not to be determined by belonging to a particular community, over and above witness to justice. That this is the case may be seen from what God said of the Arabs:

The Arabs are more stubborn in covering and hypocrisy, and apter not to know the bounds of what God has sent down on His Messenger.[14]

The reference of this statement is widened later to a universal process: group affiliation as such is to be condemned if its central content is not ethical. Of this rejection of the value of belonging on other than ethical grounds, God says:

And some of the Arabs believe in God and the Last Day, and take what they expend for offerings bringing them near to God, and the prayers of the Messenger. Surely they are an offering for them, and God will admit them into His mercy; God is All-forgiving, All-merciful.[15]

It is possible to see in these statements regarding Jews, Christians, and Arabs God calling on human being to establish a relationship with

Him as Peace (*al-Salām*). He who accepts that call is a person-of-peace (*muslim*) and his relationship with God is being-at-peace (*islam*). This call and the acceptance of it are the content of all prophecy. What God sends down to His prophets, who are people-of-peace, allows them and their followers to judge between good and evil.[16] Accepting being-at-peace as the relationship of human being as a person-of-peace and God as Peace determines our Debt to God as our Creator and the one and only Creator of everything in existence.

The Prophet the Praised was sent with this task to all people.[17] As such, he is mercy for the worlds.[18] The call was sent to every human being, regardless of affiliation, to recognize his or her existence as Debt and as determined by the agreement between us and our Maker:

God bears witness that there is no god but He—and the angels, and men possessed of knowledge—upholding justice; there is no god but He, the All-mighty, the All-wise. The true Debt to God is being-at-peace.[19]

Prophets have been sent to all peoples. They have brought them books in their languages and established rites. But they never do so, without showing that our Debt to God is being-at-peace. That is the meaning of God's comments to the Prophet the Praised:

It is He who has sent His Messenger with the guidance and the Debt of truth, that He may uplift it above every debt, though the coverers be averse.[20]

13. INTOLERANCE II

It may be recognized that God's addresses in the Recitation were directed to those who have accepted it as the call. They mention Jews, Christians, Sabaeans, Magians, and Arabs. These communities or peoples are definitively distinguished on the grounds of their members' adherence to God and righteousness. This adherence is defined as their being amongst those who are at peace (*muslims*) with regard to God as Peace (*al-Salām*) in a relationship of being-at-peace (*islam*). The person-of-peace/being-at-peace/Peace nexus cannot be restricted to one people per se. The history of each one of these peoples is full of examples of distinctions between individuals and groups who responded to the call to bear witness to justice, on the one hand, and those who rejected and went against it, on the other. Such splits have often divided neighbors and kinsfolk. Blood and other forms of close relations have not prevented ethical failure and vice versa. Strangers and unlike folk have frequently found themselves on the same side, bearing unconditional witness to justice.

It is possible to be a person-of-faith amongst any people and at any time. This is an inalienable possibility for human being as such, with God as Such. Our relationship as people-of-faith (*mu'min*) with God as Faithful (*al-Mu'min*) is faith (*iman*). This is always an individual relationship. It is entirely clear that it cannot be limited by any affiliation or lack thereof. Our comrades may belong to the peoples of the Book, but not all members of those peoples are so related.

And We cut them up into nations in the earth, some of them righteous, and some of them otherwise; and We tried them with good things and evil, that haply they should return. And they are succeeded after them a succession who inherited the Book, taking the chance goods of his lower world, and saying, "It will be forgiven us" and if chance goods the like of them come to them, they will take them. Has not the compact of the Book been taken touching them, that they should say concerning God nothing but the truth? And they have studied what is in it; and the Last Abode is better for those who are the conscious. Do you not understand? And those who hold fast to the Book, and perform the prayer—surely We leave not to waste the wage of those who set aright.[1]

Being faithful, which is a higher level than being a person-of-peace, is conditioned in such a way that it cannot be attained or satisfied by any affiliation. It is shaped by a clear and definite ethical requirement. Accepting that requirement and attaining the level of faith transforms the individual into a member of the community of the faithful and this is not to be denied on the ground of adherence to the Judaic, Christian, Sabaean, or Muslim communities. This is the community of the faithful confirmed first in virtue, and only then in everything else.

And the believers, the men and the women, are friends one of the other; they bid to honour, and forbid dishonour; they perform prayers, and pay the alms, and they obey God and His messenger.[2]

When tasked with resolving the issue of our relationship to the other, we may find a number of aspects in it. The other may be a close relative, but not a close partner in being-at-peace and belief. He or she may be at best a distant relative, but very close with regard to being-at-peace and belief. Both are possible: The person with whom relationship is established may be fundamentally different. The crucial question in each of these relationships is the question of one individual establishing relationship with another. How that individual's sense-of-self is formed also determines the content of the relationship with others. If we say we are people-of-peace (*muslim*), we may mean this in various ways. We may accept all the requirements regarding ritual, but their inner meaning may remain undiscovered to us. We may carry out the required obligations and know their meaning, but they may not be to us exclusively a means of connection with God and return to Him. Then the source of the meaning of our relations with others will come from tradition and not from consciousness of the one and the same God or from witness that there is no god but God. When tradition plays a role in our relations with others, this does not mean we will sense and know God as key witness and judge in every relationship between people.

As regards our relationship toward other and different people as a person-of-peace, both our tolerance and intolerance are based on principle, insofar as God is the source. Without Him, our relations are not grounded on principle, regardless of their quality. Human being-at-peace is relationship to God as Peace. It is a voluntary distinction in everything, including in relation to all inner and outer signs. They always speak to us of the One revealed in the many.

Tolerance is the relationship of the self to the other, where difference is suffered. In an intolerant relationship, the self does not suffer/accept difference. Such a self fears the other and hates it. Where fear and hatred are, there too is ignorance, but of a different type than the wisdom that comes from accepting that human knowledge is what allows human being to read the divine signs in the world and the self. Intolerance is determined by attitudes and behavior stimulated and sustained by fear, and so by ignorance. The "I-Thou" relationship always entails that the former knows itself better than it knows the latter. Attitudes and behavior toward the other may be derived from such knowledge alone. If the knowledge of the self, which is always conditioned and finite, is taken for absolute, then the difference of the "Thou" becomes insupportable. The "Thou" proves irreducible to the finite knowledge that takes itself for absolute. Then, fear transforms into a passion to master and destroy the "Thou." Passion is taken for a god,[3] ignorance for knowledge, the finite for the absolute.

All knowledge of the self is conditioned. It knows itself better than any "Thou." Only God knows everything, while we are given but a little knowledge. Therefore, knowledge of the self is always ignorance with regard to the Self. Each of us may say that we know ourselves better than anyone else, that no one else may know us as we do, but that God knows us better again.[4] Each self may claim to know itself much better than any "Thou," but the opposite is also true. Every "Thou" may claim to know itself as a self better than any other does. Before God, however, both self and other dispose of little knowledge.

God knows everything absolutely. Human beings are ignorant, so that every establishment of relations between them, involving the covering of God's unity or association of anything to Him, entails judgment on the basis of ignorance. That is why coming to know oneself is a limitless way of coming to know God. Not knowing ourselves is our greatest concern and the source of our fear. Such lack of self-knowledge is lack of knowledge of God. This is why fear of God stimulates and liberates. If we admit our lack of knowledge of God, we open ourselves to overcoming our lack of knowledge and our fear, and so flee from god to god. Lack of knowledge of the "Thou" is less crucial for our liberation from fear than our lack of knowledge of ourselves and of God. That is why God says to us:

> That is Satan frightening his friends, therefore do not fear them; but fear you Me, if you are believers.[5]

Whenever we are in fear of the other, it means we do not know him or her, that we have no acceptable answer as to the reasons for the differences between us and them. We do not know the meaning of the language, signs, and interpretations the other and the different deploy. In the encounter with this incomprehensibility and unreadability of everything or some part of that which determines the "Thou," the self does not recognize this as its own ignorance. To recognize our own ignorance in the "Thou" means opening up toward knowledge and freeing ourselves from ignorance. Coming to know the "Thou" means coming to know ourselves, and coming to know ourselves means coming to know God.

This means turning the self from insecurity to peace, from hatred to love, from ugliness to beauty, from arrogance to modesty, from selfishness to generosity. The opinions and behavior of the ignoramus (*jahil*) are the opposite of those of the knowing subject. The former is arrogant and brutal, the latter humble and mild.

Tolerating the other or different does not mean accepting their fears or behavior. As long as conversation with the other is possible, it should be continued. None of the participants in that conversation has a right to final judgment. And none of them is without the possibility in principle of self-realization after their authentic nature. This is why we/they are obliged to converse in good part.[6] Where discussion becomes unjust, one should turn from it toward peace.[7] When the other insults what we consider our values, we must not return the insult.[8] When attacked, so that our self, body, and community are in danger, we have the right to defense, but that too in good part, without any right to violate the dignity of the other.[9]

When the opinions or behavior of others are unacceptable, God orders the Prophet, the best example for those who bear witness, as follows:

> So, for their breaking of their compact We curse them and make their hearts hard, they pervert words from their meaning; and they have forgotten a portion of that they were reminded of; and thou wilt never cease to light upon some act of treachery on their part, except a few of them yet pardon them and forgive; surely God loves the good doers.[10]

People-of-peace may arise in every community, regardless of what external form that community takes on. Without the presence of people-of-peace, any community's faith becomes a form of idolatry and consequently of injustice. There are such people-of-peace in every community, but they are also in conflict with it. They do not accept witness that ignores God's command to be just. As such, they are vulnerable and forced to struggle. This battle, however, is nothing else than their attaining the status of people-of-peace in relationship with God as Peace.

> Many a prophet there has been with whom thousands manifold have fought, and they fainted not what smote them in God's way, neither weakened, nor did they humble themselves; and God loves the patient.[11]

The meaning of that struggle would be betrayed were its participants to forget that being-at-peace is their only debt to God. And that is what always happens when one accepts relationships with the self, with others, and with the world in which witness to Unity has faded:

> When the Messengers came unto them from before them and from behind them, saying, "Serve none but God!"[12]

The differences that are or are not tolerated remain an irreducible bond to the "Thou." It is inseparable from the boundary without which the self is impossible. Accordingly, the question of tolerance is the question of difference and boundary. Whatever the condition of the self, we can not deny our Debt. That Debt, ultimately, is our relationship with God. All of the self's relationships with other people are either covering or denial of the possibility of finding ourselves as servants, who have received everything from our Master, unless they also involve recognition of the irreducibility of the differences that abide with God.

This, our relationship as servant to God as Lord, is service. Given that we are always before a God we cannot see, but Who sees us, we are always potentially coverers (unbelievers or idolaters), insofar as we accept remoteness and nearness, interiority and exteriority as particulars. Our selves are torn between that which covers and that which discovers. Our dialogue with God takes place with due respect for the various possibilities within us, for those conditions of the self which cover and the self's inherent predisposition toward return of the debt to the eternal and only God:

> Say, "O coverers, I serve not what you serve, and you are not serving what I serve, nor am I serving what you have served, neither are you serving what I serve. To you your Debt, and to me my Debt!"[13]

As communities of believers, jews and christians have everything muslims do—their prophets, their revelations, and the possibility of redemption. In all these three sacred communities, acknowledged by God, the key value is human perfectibility. In the muslim's quest for human perfection, as he or she approximates his or her most sublime potential, he or she may be tempted to consider these others "friends" regardless of their obligation to affirm their affiliation through virtue, because of similarity alone. Friendship with them, however, insofar as it does not involve witness to righteousness, can mean losing the perspective in which everything reveals and bears witness to God alone, and that is and must be paramount. This is why God's call to the faithful not to take even Jews and Christians for friends, which is the same as His call not to consider one's brother or father as friends, is the general requirement that just witness not be conditioned in any way beyond our covenant with God, not even by a feeling of close-ness, kinship, or profound similarity. Consequently, friendship, even with our own children, brothers and sisters, or the religious communi-ties closest to us, the Jews and Christians, is possible only through God, but not only is it possible through God, it is a necessary conse-quence of authentic being-at-peace. Thus, we are again called to con-fess there is no god but God and that nothing or no one, no matter how attractive or close it or he seems, may condition or alter that wit-ness, be he Jew or Christian, father or brother:

> O believers, take not your fathers and brothers
> to be your friends, if they prefer covering to belief;
> whosoever of you takes them for friends, those—
> they are the evildoers.[14]

14. THE MUSLIM

During the last two centuries of the second Christian millennium, that part of humanity which calls itself and others call "Muslim" has frequently found itself the subject of major suffering. The killing and persecution of Muslims and the destruction of their property have taken place from the Balkans in the west to the foothills of the Himalayas in the east, from the Central Asian steppes in the north to the equatorial jungles of Africa in the south. Nor is there much hope that this suffering will soon stop. It has been the subject of much investigation and interpretation.[1] There is, however, something missing in these approaches to one of the greatest tragedies in human existence, which is the clear discrimination of two points of view—the external and the internal—as well as the two languages advocating them. Doing so would make clear the lack of a *lingua franca* for relations between entrenched and combative subjects of difference.[2]

Current interpretation of the concepts of *muslim* and *islam* takes place almost entirely either through the lens of Western culture or unenlightened denial. It is challenging, and perhaps liberating, to look at the phenomena signified by these terms without that lens. This requires that the concepts be investigated thoroughly to clarify the differences in the roles they play in traditional intellectuality and modern

ideologies.³ This is crucial both for Muslims and for those who see
nothing in that name that touches them.⁴

At the heart of these considerations lie questions regarding the
grounds for tolerance and attempts by Muslims to justify intolerance.
Attention has been drawn to the normative and interpretative determination of the sense-of-self that is called "Muslim" by those in the
faith and by others. The current interpretation community of Muslims
and their self-understandings represent a very wide range of individual senses-of-self in societies across the world, with different linguistic, semiotic, and semantic ranges, lumped together in a very unclear
whole called the "Muslim world."

. Both approaches are consequences of complicated historical, political, and economic circumstances. These approaches accept, directly
and/or indirectly, textual complexes they consider fundamental and a
certain content as decisive for their formation. The presence of these
texts—and above all the *Qur'an*, its interpretation, and the books of
Hadith—differs from one society to another. These differences cannot
anywhere or at any time be excluded entirely. Their presence is incor-
porated in interpretations that are, in the modern world, inseparable
from dominant ideological worldviews, to which are related simplify-
ing descriptions of the complex archipelago of civilization. Throughout this process, it is not uncommon for similarities to be overstressed
and differences ignored.

There is a general feeling that the concept of *muslim* is clear and
obvious. This feeling of clarity, which is itself far from transparent,
has been introduced into nearly all contemporary discussion. Given
the obvious cases of loss of moral foundation on the part of individual
and collective subjects, conditioned by this sense of knowing that informs the subject, it is worth attempting a sort of deconstruction of
the concept and the semantic fields it belongs to or is forced into.

Two elements clearly play a decisive role in forming people who,
either individually or collectively, consider themselves Muslims. The
first consists of the holy texts and their course through history. The
second element consists of a very wide range of cultural particularities. Given that the Prophet, the *Qur'an*, and the *Hadith* were
originally (or for the most part) situated in an Arabic environment, it

is not easy to determine and maintain the boundary between the mus-
lim/islamic in the general sense and what is contingently Muslim due
to the Arab environment. However the task has been resolved, the
common core takes on different meanings, connections, and tensions
in its various cultural environments.

The noun *muslim*, with its feminine form and plural, occurs in the
Recitation forty-two times. A superficial glance at usage easily confirms that its reference is not limited to a particular community or
time. It signifies a condition of humanity, inseparable from human nature as such. That this is so may be seen from certain examples of
how the term is used in the Recitation. One must relate these examples, however, to all the other terms, verbs, and nouns that together
make up a single semantic field—forty-nine appearances of the noun
salām (peace), twenty-two appearances of the verb *aslama* (to be at
peace), and seven appearances of the term *islam* (being-at-peace), all
derived from the verbal root *slm*.

The term *muslim* may be understood in its original meaning only
when it has been restored to this semantic field:

And who speaks fairer than he who calls unto God and does
righteousness and says, "Surely I am of them who are the people-of-peace."[5]

And Abraham charged his sons with this and Jacob likewise,
"My sons, God has chosen for you the Debt; see that you die
not save as a person-of-peace."[6]

Moses said, "O my people, if you believe in God, in Him put
your trust, if you are people-of-peace."[7]

"O my Lord, Thou hast given me to rule, and Thou hast taught
me the interpretation of tales. O Thou, the Originator of the
heavens and earth, Thou art my Protector in this world and the
next. O receive me to Thee in true peace, and join me with the
righteous."[8]

And when I inspired the Apostles, "Believe in Me and My Messenger"; they said, "We believe; witness Thou that we are at
Peace."[9]

Say, "The Holy Spirit brought it down from thy Lord in truth, and to confirm those who believe, and to be a guidance and good tidings to those who seek Peace."[10]

Say, "My prayer, my ritual sacrifice, my living, my dying—all belongs to God, the Lord of all Being. No associate has He. Even so I have been commanded, and I am the first of the people-of-peace."[11]

In the Recitation, God's call to us to establish appropriate relations with each other is effected by the order to offer or appeal for *salām*. As already mentioned, the term *salām* belongs to the same semantic field as *muslim*. We will give only some of the strongest examples of its use in the Recitation:

He is God; there is no god but He. He is the knower of the Unseen and the Visible; He is the All-merciful, the Ever-merciful. He is God; there is no god but He. He is the King, the All-holy, the Peace, the All-faithful, the All-preserver, the All-mighty, the All-compeller, the All-sublime. Glory be to God, above that they associate! He is God, the Creator, the Maker, the Shaper. To Him belong the Names Most Beautiful. All that is in the heavens and the earth magnifies Him; He is the All-mighty, the All-wise.[12]

The servants of the All-merciful are those who walk in the earth modestly and who, when the ignorant address them, say, "Peace."[13]

People of the Book, now there has come to you Our Messenger, making clear to you many things you have been concealing of the Book, and effacing many things. There has come to you from God a light, and a Book Manifest whereby God guides whosoever follows His good pleasure in the ways of Peace, and brings them forth from the shadows into the light by His leave; and He guides them to an upright path.[14]

Surely those who believe, and do deeds of righteousness, their Lord will guide them for their belief; beneath them rivers flowing in gardens of bliss; their cry therein, "Glory to Thee, O God," their greeting, "Peace," and their cry ends, "Praise belongs to God, the Lord of all Being."[15]

Those to whom We gave the Book before this believe in it and when it is recited to them, they say, "We believe in it; surely it is the truth from our Lord. Indeed, even before it we were at Peace." These shall be given their wage twice over for that they patiently endured, and avert evil with good, and expend of that We have provided them. When they hear idle talk, they turn away from it and say, "We have our deeds, and you your deeds. Peace be upon you! We desire not the ignorant."[16]

And for his saying, "My Lord, surely these are a people who believe not"—yet pardon them, and say, "Peace!" soon they will know.[17]

O believers, when you are journeying in the path of God, be discriminating, and do not say to him who offers you Peace, "Thou art not a believer," seeking the chance goods of the present life.[18]

What is the ultimate meaning of the term *al-Salām*? And why is it so crucial for relations between people that the Prophet said, "I swear by the One who controls my life that you will not enter Heaven unless you have faith. You will not have faith unless you love each other. Do you want me to tell you what to do to love each other? Just invoke peace one upon the other?"[19] Answers to these questions are be found in the Recitation, where Peace (*al-Salām*) is one of God's beautiful names.[20]

God is *al-Salām*. The whole human dilemma lies in voluntary return to Him. He who seeks *salām* and determines himself by it is *muslim*. *Salām* is our highest goal. All the things of the world are signs through which Peace reveals itself. Our knowledge of them is recognition of Peace in them and in ourselves. Our remembrance of God is primarily of Him as Peace.[21] Peace is our relationship to ourselves, the world, and God. The relationship of the muslim or seeker of peace and God as Peace is *islam*.[22] This is shown clearly by all the verses in the Recitation in which the concept is mentioned:

> Today I have fashioned your Debt for you, and I have completed My blessing upon you, and I have approved being-at-peace for your debt.[23]
>
> The true debt to God is being-at-peace. Those who were given the Book were not at variance except after the knowledge came to them, being insolent one to another.[24]
>
> Whoso desires another Debt than being-at-peace, it shall not be accepted of him; in the next world he shall be among the losers.[25]
>
> Is he whose breast God has expanded unto being-at-peace, so he walks in a light from his Lord. . . . But woe to those whose hearts are hardened against the remembrance of God! Those are in manifest error.[26]
>
> Whomsoever God desires to guide He expands his breast to being-at-peace; whomsoever He desires to lead astray, He makes his breast narrow, tight, as if he were climbing to heaven.[27]
>
> And who does greater evil than he who forges against God falsehood, when he is called to be at Peace?[28]
>
> They count it as a favour to thee that they have been at Peace! Say, "Do not count your being-at-peace as a favour to me; nay, but rather God confers a favour upon you, in that He has guided you to belief, if it be that you are truthful."[29]

Viewed from a muslim point-of-view, witness to Unity is crucial to the formation of each and any self. The One reveals Itself through His names. Every sense-of-self stands between a twofold distinction of the names—those of wrath, which manifest in the aspect of distance from the One, and the names of mercy, which manifest in closeness to Him. Given that mercy surpasses wrath, our response to God's call to self-realization in His names,[30] which is also His call to human being to requite evil with good,[31] may be demonstrated using the example of our relationship to God through five of the often mentioned ninety-nine names of God:

God is *al-Salām (Peace)*. We who turn toward God as Peace take into or discover in ourselves peace to become people-of-peace. Our relationship as people-of-peace to God as Peace is being-at-peace or *islam*.

God is *al-Mu'min (Faithful)*. We who turn to God as the Faithful take on or discover in ourselves His attribute and become faithful. Our relationship as such to God as Such is faith or faithfulness *(iman)*.

God is *al-Muhsin (the Maker of beauty)*. When we relate to God as the Maker of the beautiful, we too are *muhsin*. Our relationship as makers of beauty or doers of good to God as the Maker of beauty and Doer of good is beauty and the good *(ihsan)*.

God is *al-Halim (the Clement)*. When we turn toward Him as the Clement, we take into or find in ourselves His name and become clement. Our relationship as clement to God as Clement is clemency *(hilm)*.

God is *al-Hamid (the All-praised)*. We who turn to God as Such take into or find in ourselves the name the All-praised and are praised and, so, praising. Our relationship as praised or praising *(Muhammad)* to God as All-praised is praise *(hamd)*. This is one more expression of our highest capacity, as the Praised is our best model.

One could expand these examples of our self-realization in and through God's names to cover all of His beautiful names. But, we are creatures whose place in the totality of existence is on earth. Our knowledge of God is through our relationship with the divine signs in the world and our own self. Being peaceful, faithful, beautiful, and clement toward the things in creation, we discover and confess that they are created in truth and that each of them bears witness to some one of God's names. This recognition of right in everything in the world and in the inner life of the recognizer is a condition of human dignity.

15. THE UNIVERSALITY OF PROPHECY

No aspect of the Jewish, Christian, or Islamic traditions can be discussed without recognizing the crucial role of prophecy for the viewpoint as a whole. All statements from the Recitation considered in this text as binding effective utterances interact with sense-of-self. Their very presence in the sense-of-self is interpretation. No sense-of-self can be frozen and unchanging with regard to itself. It simply cannot. That does not mean that the sense-of-self is not susceptible to the allure of such a possibility. The question arises: What importance do, or should, the verses of the Recitation have for change in the sense-of-self?

This question may be answered in a variety of ways. We who seek to answer it are pupils or disciples. Our goal is learning or knowledge of the sense-of-self. We seek to learn or study ourselves. Our relationship as learners to the goal, that about which we want to learn or study, is learning or study. The teachers, or those who know, are within us. They are available through their pupils who have become teachers and comprise a chain of tradition.

Simple reception of the transmitted is not enough, however. The prophet is a teacher who has not received knowledge from human being. Knowledge has been sent down into the heart of his innermost and best faculty. He has realized the knowledge of the Highest in himself, for he is His messenger. Both before and after this, the prophet ate and drank, walked amongst people, and talked with them. When problems appear with conditions and tendencies in a given society, how the majority of selves in that society have been formed becomes a crucial issue. It is decisive for any change desired after a given model. The models are the perfect people—prophets and saints. Every society is enlightened by such fully realized people. They always exist in society, or even alone, as their self-realization is their connection with God and consciousness of the Debt to Him. The human sense-of-self, accordingly, finds itself between two extremes—the highest, toward which God directs it, and the lowest, toward which the Devils tempt it.

One might say of existence as a whole that it is a partition between Unity and void. Unity is manifest through creation or existence. In so manifesting, His essence neither falls short nor exceeds. All existence manifests Him in the simultaneity of His remoteness and nearness, majesty and beauty, severity and gentleness. All things belong simultaneously to two levels—a higher and a lower. This belonging, however, is conditional: what is lower in one relationship is higher in another.

Existence as a whole contains infinite levels of being. It is possible on each of them to find revelation of the One. He reveals Himself in everything, while also hiding in everything. That there is no god but God means that He is revealed in every sign, without ever being that sign itself. He is and is not in everything. He is because there is no reality beyond Him. He is not, as through manifestation He appears in relationship to void.

Creation reveals the names of God. There is nothing in all of creation that does not reveal. Everything is a sign closer to the One on one side, further on the other, and so closer to multiplicity and void. That which makes it closer also reveals that it belongs to the partition. By drawing close, things realize or show themselves in their relationship with the One. By drawing away, they deny themselves and touch void. Lastly, all existence is divided between Intellect, as the created treasure house of all knowing, and void, against which this knowing reveals itself in an infinite movement of distantiation and dispersion. We, humankind, are the gathering of all creation. In us are gathered the names dispersed through the worlds. We are divided between body and Spirit. Whatever the level of our existence, our sense of self involves being "in between." For human being, self-realization lies in the return to the One or acceptance of the Self—as there is no self but the Self—and in severing the link of the self with the non-Self.

When we realize or discover the divine names in ourselves, we return to perfect creaturehood or our purpose. Divine creation is perfect, and we know it when we realize our original and authentic perfection. In this way, we become revealed images of God and most beautiful uprightness. Our potential is shown in the totality of existence and realized in the prophets and the saints, who represent what human being as such is capable of. The prophets in every place and at every time turn to God. They are on the upright path and ceaselessly recall God and call on Him, refusing in this way any connection with the non-Real. The prophets and the saints are, however, always related to other people. They walk amongst us and talk our language. For this reason the prophets and the saints are the best exemplars of total obedience, sublime calm, and so forth. Through the prophets, God reveals His books and instructions, which confirm their virtues—generosity and obedience. They are realized through a return to God or *loci* in which He has revealed Himself.

All existence is divided between heaven and earth. Everything is situated between these two extremes. They are connected by the axes of ascent and descent. So it is with human being: We, too, are divided between body and Spirit on the upright path of discovering God's image or most beautiful uprightness. Our highest possibility is ascent toward God and closeness to Him. But there are always three possibilities: to take the upright path toward peace or the path of the blessed, to take the opposite path toward void, or to wander on a single level of existence. This is contained in the Opening (*al-Fatihah*):

> Thee only we serve; to Thee alone we pray for succour: Guide
> us unto the upright path, the path of those whom Thou hast

blessed, not of those against whom Thou art wrathful, nor of those who are astray!

For human being to take the upright path, we must first confess the conditioned nature of our sense-of-self and the possibility of discovering authentic perfection. This conversion stimulates us to turn from a lower toward a higher level of being, or to distinguish lower from higher and cleave to the higher, in the openness of the road toward the Absolute. This is not an unconditional possibility for every individual. The presence of the perfected human being—God's prophets and messengers—testifies to that. The traveler always set his sights by them. We accept one so that we may hear his clearly intelligible discourse. Adherence to one prophet entails acceptance of all. Of the one chosen as model, the others—known and unknown—all speak. They all testify of each other. But no prophet is the goal of our journeying. He is just the guide to the One who is the reference of the act of witness that there is no self but the Self. The One may be approached through the doors opened by the Prophet through his realization of that testimony.

Binding to and approximation toward the Prophet is our desire to realize in ourselves the Name that gathers all names. That Name is God (*Allah*, in Arabic). He may be called by that name, as by all of His beautiful names. Our self-realization is the attainment of our finest nature, which is to establish relationship with God through His beautiful names: the person-of-peace with Peace through being-at-peace; the faithful with the Faithful through faith; the praised with the All-praised through praise; the beautiful with the Beautiful through beauty; the anointed with the Anointer through anointing; and so forth, through all the beautiful names revealed by the world and the perfect human being.

Prophecy is how God offers guidance to human beings through human mediation. Just as divine mercy surpasses His wrath, so divine guidance surpasses His temptation. Without temptation, which is incarnate in Satan, the messages of the prophets would be without sense. Without distance, there can be no closeness; without wrong, no right;

without darkness, no perception of the light. All the differences that allow the cosmos to exist depend on the variety and distinction of God's qualities. On the moral and spiritual level, variety comes to be revealed through the forms of guidance and election, which are represented by the Prophet and Satan.[1]

To be Satan means to be an enemy of the prophets, as God says in the Recitation:

> So We have appointed to every Prophet an enemy—satans of men and jinn, revealing tawdry speech to each other, all as a delusion; yet, had thy Lord willed, they would never have done it. So leave them to their forging, and that the hearts of those who believe not in the world to come may incline to it, and that they may be well-pleased with it, and that they may gain what they are gaining.[2]

Temptation is a universal phenomenon that people encounter throughout their existence, from first to last. Temptation exists in the external world and in our selves. So does guidance. We cannot be understood apart from our being between prophet and Satan or without confirming that our innermost nature is determined by witness of Unity. This is because we are shaped by free will received from God. We were created in God's image (sura), as was the world as a whole, and as the Recitation was revealed. God's qualities are gathered in human being, including free will. Only with this quality can we be confident with God, in which state God as the Creator and we as creatures are faithful. That God is Faithful in His covenant of confidence is an unvarying attribute. In the case of human being, being faithful is an expression of our highest capacity.

God created us with His own two hands.[3] This means that we can choose His right hand, guidance, or His left hand, temptation. Without this possibility of choice, people would not be able to receive confidence.

The fundamental content of the message received and related by the prophets is witness to divine Unity. According to the divine revelation in the Recitation, all the prophets have received and testified to the One:

And We sent never a Messenger before thee except that We revealed to him, saying, "There is no god but I; so serve Me."[4]

Each prophet received and bore witness to this universal message of Unity as well as to his own mission. In the case of the prophet Muhammad, this testimony is gathered in the expression, "There is no god but God, and Muhammad is His servant and His messenger." Given that all the messengers were sent to particular areas and times, amongst people of a particular nation, their reception and transmission of their self-witness have always differed. God speaks of this in the Recitation:

Every nation has its Messenger.[5]

We have sent no Messenger save with tongue of his people.[6]

To every one of you We have appointed a right way and an open road.[7]

If we consider the multitude of God's prophets sent to us at various times and places, with one and the same message, using the example of the Torah and the *Qur'an*, we may confirm God's guarantee of translatability from one language to another. God's prophets, whose sayings are included in these revelations, spoke in different languages, but everything any of them said in the Books is contained in each of those languages. Accepting any one of the prophets means confessing the possibility that, regardless of the peculiarities of language, every individual and every nation may find in that prophet the best example of journeying toward God. In each of them, as a speaker of a particular language, the discourse of all the others is translated, through their connection with Unity.

Testifying to divine Unity and Muhammad's prophethood entails acceptance of all the prophets, regardless of the differences between them. Beyond all their differences, the essence of their conception and transmission or relation of witness is one and the same. Given that human being has only interpretation of this essential Unity, the prophetic heritage is in an infinite multiplicity of linguistic, symbolic, and interpretative systems. This is the sense of God's command:

Say you, "We believe in God, and in that which has been sent down on us and sent down on Abraham, Ishmael, Isaac and Jacob, and the Tribes, and that which was given to Moses and Jesus and the Prophets, of their Lord; we make no division between any of them, and in Him we find our Peace."[8]

This confession relates to the essence of prophecy, which appears differently in each case. The differences between prophets are determined by the conditions in which they acted and the messages they received and related. The languages, signs, and meanings that condition each of the peoples are sufficient to receive the prophetic message without betraying its essential unity, in spite of all the differences. This means that witness to the Unity of God is translatable into all linguistic, symbolic, and semantic systems, as a treasure for all people.

16. THE NATION OF THE JUST

God is One. The revelation of Unity in creation is possible only in the many, which neither determines nor supplements that Unity. All existence—heaven, earth, and everything between—is an inexhaustible inscription of that Unity. It appears from absolute nearness to infinite remoteness. Everything that appears in this way in the external world is a revelation of Unity and is so through the unlimited multiplicity of division and dispersion. Thus, the One is manifest in multiplicity, showing Himself in every individual, while also remaining outside.

The whole of existence is revelation of fullness in relation to the void. Existence is absolute, as it is with the Absolute. But it is also void, as revelation takes place against it. Everything scattered across the worlds is strung between light and dark, heaven and earth. Due to creation itself, it is not full of light, but it is nothing else either. What is strung across the worlds from heaven to earth in this way gathers in human being between Spirit and body. These ranges of existence in the world and in us correspond to each other.

The world is human being-in-large, while human being is the world-in-little. Both contain countless signs that reveal the truth. All the signs comprise multiple connected levels of existence, from the Absolute to the void. Self-realization means to return from the void as the extreme of multiplicity toward the One as the Principle of all existence.

When we have realized Unity in ourselves and our nature has become a showing of the beautiful divine names, we are fullness of divine manifestation—His image or beautiful uprightness. Such a one is God's prophet and one of the good, one to whom God has revealed the reason and purpose of creation and who expresses this message, translating it from inner core into character and language.

If one is to understand the reasons for our relations toward the world in the traditional point-of-view, one must accept the prophets and their books in full seriousness. But, there have always been, and no doubt will always be, different relations to the prophets, as God too says:

> Indeed, We sent Messengers before thee, among the factions of the ancients, and not a single Messenger came to them, but they mocked at him.[1]

Recognizing the One in the many is the return of existence to its uncreated Principle. There may be nothing in creation that is not in the original manifold. That first and ultimate Unity in which everything that is in existence is gathered reveals Him in the names of things. These names are strung across the heavens and the earth and everything between, but they are gathered in human being. God, who gathers in Himself all His names, may be addressed in various ways. Given that this address is made out of difference, the names too differ. Some correspond to closeness and mercy, others to remoteness and wrath. Everything in existence is determined by the relationship between these names. God, however, says through the Prophet: "My mercy surpasses My wrath."[2] The meaning of doctrine, ritual, and virtue is our return to God, from remoteness to nearness, from anger to mercy, from darkness to light. Our witness to Unity allows each phenomenon to admit the truth that is in it and human being to realize itself in Truth, Faithfulness, and Beauty. Given that there is nowhere one can flee from God, this is flight to Him and seeking refuge in His mercy. His mercy is all-comprehending,[3] as is His knowledge.[4]

God's knowledge comprehends all, while to us is given only a little of that knowledge, as He says in the Recitation:

> They will question thee concerning the Spirit. Say, "The spirit is of the bidding of my Lord. You have been given of knowledge nothing except a little."[5]

Reception of the Spirit into the core of the sense-of-self is an authentic possibility for us. This is connection with God through the Spirit. But the Spirit is at God's command and so it is the expression of full freedom. It cannot be subjected to any command but God's. That command comes with full knowledge. Every human attempt to command the Spirit converts our little knowledge into an illusion of fullness and God's absolute knowledge into the illusion of deficiency. That is blasphemy of the Spirit—unforgivable sin,[6] which in its ultimate significance is the same as association unto God.[7] God's will is entirely free. Human will is too, insofar as God allows it, because of the covenant between them. Openness and humility, whose core expression is being-at-peace, allow us to prepare for reception of the Spirit as harmonization of our limited will with the Absolute through witness that there is no will except the Will. The relationship between human being and God does not deny the Unity of the Real. The human ability to know is a gift from God, Who has absolute knowledge. This relationship is God's will. He speaks in and through it: "O men, you are the ones that have need of God; He is the All-sufficient, the All-laudable."[8]

Therefore one may say that our self-realization is the discovery in our own character of the names of closeness, mercy, and knowledge. Given that knowledge and mercy are present in everything, dependent on the degree of realization, we divide into three general groups— those on the right, those on the left, and those who have progressed on the road compared to the others.[9] None of them is limited territorially, racially, or linguistically, although they are always members of linguistic and historical communities. They belong to communities in which a multitude of differences gather. These people are a community inside the community. They share the knowledge of our inexpungeable debt to God, which depends neither on language nor on time period but may be demonstrated in all of them. They are the Just in every nation. They bear witness that we are all born with the same portion of suitability and openness for good and beauty, for the road to the One and to the knowledge of Him.

Each of these communities has an authentic capacity for discovery of the names of closeness and mercy and for bringing them to realization in human individuality, which neither is nor can be determined by a particular form. These communities, built by open individuals, are holy communities of the Lord. At their heart is the Unity with which every one of these individuals establishes a relationship through free will in order to realize in the sense-of-self His revelation through the names of remoteness and closeness, majesty and beauty. In that core, there can be nothing but God as the Name that gathers all names. Thus the road to realization in the Absolute is open to every individual in that community.

In the Recitation, God shows clearly that the multiplicity and diversity of peoples is His sign. Belonging to any one of them, regardless of by what and how the group was formed, is neither hindrance nor advantage in redemption or return to God. In each of these groups, regardless of by what or how its consciousness was formed, there is always a distinction between those turned toward the Absolute and those turned toward the void, and also between those who see signs of Unity in all things and never take anything in the world or themselves for a god beside God. These orientations differ. Given that the prophets called on all people to turn to the One, those who have done so represent a factor of differentiation within the community. Whenever censure is pronounced on a group—Jews or Christians, for example—it cannot apply to the entire community. In each such group, there is distinction—between the just and unjust, the mindful and the oblivious. The person-of-peace is required to determine and maintain relations with other people, if only his or her parents and children, on the basis of connection with the One.

> Had they performed the Torah and the Gospel, and what was sent down to them from their Lord, they would have eaten both what was above them, and what was beneath their feet. Some of them are a just nation; but many of them—evil are the things they do.[10]

Yet they are not all alike; some of the People of the Book are a nation upstanding, that recite God's signs in the watches of the night, bowing themselves. Believing in God and in the Last Day, bidding to honour and forbidding dishonour, vying one with the other in good works; those are of the righteous. And whatsoever good you do, you shall not be denied the just reward of it; and God knows the conscious.[11]

And of the People of the Book is he who, if thou trust him with a hundredweight, will restore it to thee; and of them is he who, if thou trust him with one pound, will not restore it thee, unless ever thou standest over him.[12]

The people(s) of the Book belong to different times, places, languages, and races. In any group, the Just are apart. They distinguish truth from falsehood and adhere to it, forming one community in spite of their multiplicity. One may say of them that they realize themselves in their return to God or being on the road of valid witness: There is no peace except Peace, no faith except Faith, no beauty except Beauty, and so forth through all the beautiful names of God.

The ways to God are many. They are varied, but they all reach the divine Unity that surpasses and encompasses all plurality. Everything else is inferior to Him. Return to Him is ascent. Goodness and beauty reveal and testify to that return, as does being just. Is it not true that the response of some Christians to the suffering of the Jews, and vice versa, testifies clearly to the presence of the Just in every people?[13]

The citations from the divine Revelation represent the peoples of the Book as seen from the point-of-view of the people of the Recitation. Given the equivalence in principle of the prophets and the revealed books, an equally valid view may be taken of "Muslims." Their being a just people depends on how they have received the Recitation and that which has been sent down to them. But they are not and cannot be homogenous. Some of them are an upright nation, "that recite God's signs in the watches of the night, bowing themselves. Believing in God and in the Last Day, bidding to honour and forbidding dishonour, vying one with the other in good works."

A near infinity of means may be discerned whereby the community of the Just is elected. None of those means is enough because they are deployed by wayfarers returning to the One in which fullness of human self-realization lies. The closer their character is to unity, beauty, and mercy, the closer the names are. In this way, their witness to justice or recognition of the rights of everything that is in existence is realized, as the Prophet says, "So you should give the rights of all those who have a right on you."[14] Through such confession, we allow closeness and mercy to appear in ourselves as the right to return and our return to the One to appear as the right to closeness and mercy. Progress on that road is witnessed to by beauty of character. In such a character, means and end are clearly differentiated. Means are various, but the end is one—the discovery of humanity in all its potential. A beautiful character or virtue is always beyond means—whether doctrine or ritual. God speaks of this in the Recitation:

> It is not piety, that you turn your faces to the East and to the West. True piety is this: to believe in God, and the Last Day, the angels, the Book, and the Prophets, to give of one's substance, however cherished, to kinsmen, and orphans, the needy, the traveller, beggars, and to ransom the slave, to perform the prayer, to pay the alms. and they who fulfill their covenant when they have engaged in a covenant, and endure with fortitude misfortune, hardship and peril, these are they who are true in their faith, these are the truly conscious.[15]

We become thereby more conscious of our Debt, as mercy and knowledge reside with God. If we partake of them, they have been received into us by coming to know the self. Those who have only that which they received and have received only what are the names of God are a just people who confess that there is a counterpart to all apparent forms of closeness, worldly fortune, kith and kin, fate and flesh, self-hood and heart. For them, recognition of right in everything that exists is a form of witness to the One and rejection of forgetting.

17. DIALOGUE

Our intentions toward and dialogue with the other shape our consciousness of our Debt to God. We have nothing we have not received. Consciousness of that transforms all our property into debt and us into God's debtors. That Debt, according to this tradition, consists of four things—being-at-peace (*islam*), faith (*iman*), doing good and beautiful things (*ihsan*), and recognizing the fullness of the Hour (*sa'a*). These are the relations of human being as such to God as Such:

> The person-of-peace (*muslim*)—being-at-peace (*islam*)—Peace (*al-Salām*);
> The person-of-faith (*mu'min*)—faith (*iman*)—the Faithful (*al-Mu'min*);
> The doer of good and beauty (*muhsin*)—doing good and beautiful things (*ihsan*)—the Doer of good and beauty (*al-Muhsin*).

Each of these human possibilities—the person-of-peace, the person-of-faith, and the doer of good or beauty—is relationship toward God to Whom belong the most beautiful names. Each of these three expressions is relationship to God through one of His beautiful names: Peace, the Faithful, the Doer of Good and Beauty. These three aspects—being-at-peace, faith, and doing beautiful things—correspond to three questions: what, why, and how?

Through these questions, our authentic nature is realized, as shown by God's command:

And do good, as God has been good to thee![1]

But be good-doers; God loves the good-doers.[2]

Insofar as we are peaceful, faithful, and doers of beauty, we realize in ourselves the corresponding divine name: Peace, the Faithful, the Doer of Good and Beauty:

If you do good, it is your own souls you do good to.[3]

And who is there that has a fairer debt than he who submits his will to God, being a good-doer.[4]

Dispute not with the People of the Book save in the fairer manner, except for those of them that do wrong; and say, "We believe in what has been sent down to us, and what has been sent down to you; our God and your God is One, and in Him we have found Peace."[5]

Many of the people of the Book wish they might restore you as coverers, after you have believed, in the jealousy of their souls, after the truth has become clear to them; yet do you pardon and be forgiving, till God brings His command; truly God is powerful over everything.[6]

Being-at-peace, faith, and doing beauty are ways we actualize our confession that there is no god but God. In each encounter with the world as a whole and with each individual thing, we confess that God is both near and far, merciful and wrathful. Recollecting God reveals the truth in both. If we do not recognize right in those things, then they appear to us spoiled. That is our view of things, but God made nothing without a purpose. Every human relationship with the self and the world becomes, in like manner, spoiled and damned, like the world and everything in it, if it is not our purpose to return to God or confess that His Face is always before us, wherever we turn.

We are created beings and learn about ourselves through the world and other people. Our being created directs us toward our Creator, as source and purpose, for God is, in the end, the Creator of everything, including us and what we do.

That is why God commands us that, even in relation to our enemies, we urge Peace and confess before them:

> The servants of the All-merciful are those who walk in the earth modestly and who, when the ignorant address them, say, "Peace."[7]

Our ability to know and to "grow" in that knowledge testifies to the openness of our core toward absolute knowledge and our preadaptation for return to the One. Everything that we may experience as humans on that path of return is created or testimony to creaturehood. It always both is and is not. It is, for there is nothing that is not created with Truth; it is not, for nothing may be of itself and for itself independently of Truth. Human learning takes place through all the things in our environment, amongst which are all other people. The possibility that this may be entails the openness and pre-adaptation of the learner that everything outside of us may be gathered in us. For this reason, listening, speaking, and reading are ways of our coming to know ourselves.

This lesson cannot be limited, for creaturehood does not limit the Creator. It is not possible in any way to deny creaturehood with Truth. When that is denied, things become spoiled, for their ground is in the limited or void, and so they are truly without ground. Confessing the Truth of the creaturehood of everything entails ceaseless dialogue, as a means of reading the signs in the world and in ourselves, which is infinite approach to Mercy and retreat from Wrath, approach to Peace and retreat from non-Peace. Everything in the external world reveals one of God's names, and human self-realization is the knowing of them all. That is the reason for limitless conversation and dialogue as the path to Unity, to which nothing may be associated or joined.

> Say, "People of the Book! Come now to a word common between us and you, that we serve none but God, and that we associate not aught with Him, and do not some of us take others as Lords, apart from God." And if they turn their backs, say, "Bear witness that we are people-of-peace."[8]

Whenever we take something or someone besides God as our ground, it becomes our master. In the connection between us as admitting and the ground as known, the relationship is service. The ground always gives and so indebts the recipient. Our relationships to the other are determined by our relationship to the ground. Given that the ground determines the values, rules, and behavior of its subordinate, every attack on it will be experienced as threatening both the ground and its servant. While we may be related to God as the Ground, this does not mean that the relationship cannot change. It must be maintained and strengthened. Doctrine, ritual, and virtue are the only means to do that.

Debt is the relationship of human being as indebted to God as Indebting. The confidence offered by God and received by us requires free will. There is no constraint in the Debt. There is always a risk, however, that we may see the indebting in other people or in the world as a whole. We may return our Debt to God, however, through our relationships to ourselves, others, and the world. Each self is dependent on Him from Whom we received, but only to the same degree as every other self. This dependence may never be excluded and no "vision" of God is ever finally achieved redemption of the Debt. This is why it is asked of us that we strengthen our security, but also that we be clement toward others:

> Abuse not those to whom they pray, apart from God, or they will abuse God in revenge without knowledge.[9]

Our openness to interpretation of the signs in the world, which we access through listening, looking, touch, and smell, testifies that all our knowledge is little and that we will never complete the process of coming to know. Everything we know regarding the earthly signs has been sent down from a higher world, that it might be witnessed. This is the relationship of earth and heaven or body and Spirit. None of this speaks to anything but the Unity of the Creator. If human being does not know that, then our knowledge stems from void and the signs are inverted: They cease to be close to their creaturehood with Truth; between us and them, there yawns an unbridgeable chasm.

Given constant openness to the attainment of knowledge, which becomes part of our being, we may say that of all people we know ourselves best. But even that knowledge is little. When the knowledge is of other people, with whom we are in contact, we may say that we always know less of them than they do of themselves, but also that they know themselves better than anyone else. Given that the process of gaining knowledge is unlimited for every individual, our preoccupation with ignorance is a crucial and sufficient concern, as Imam Ali says:

He who claims is ruined and he who concocts falsehood is disappointed. He who opposes right with his face gets destruction. It is enough ignorance for a man not to know himself. He who is strong rooted in piety does not get destruction, and the plantation of a people based on piety never remains without water. Hide yourselves in your houses and reform yourselves. Repentance is at your back. One should praise only God and condemn only his own self.[10]

We are open to knowledge, but all we can attain is less than complete knowledge. Our authentic and original creaturehood means that our knowledge and ignorance are always less than complete. It may be said that each time and place is different from any other existential mode. There is an irreducible difference. The relationship between that knowledge and the Absolute is nil. It is wisdom to confess the impossibility of knowing God but also to admit that nothing can be known as real without the Real. These differences are not maintained like "a graven image," but a continuous conversation with the other and different, which, as participants in the many, reveal divine Unity, along with all the other signs in the world and the self.

Dialogue and difference are conditions of our return to God or self-realization in knowledge. Whatever difference may be discerned between people, God is the fundamental other in that relationship. Because human being may be reduced to quantitative form and openness denied, and given that the negation of human being is always also denial of the Creator, difference cannot be resolved apart from God as always and everywhere present. There can be no human dialogue of which God is not witness, nor any difference between participants in a dialogue which God does not finally inform. When members of a community of the Book are involved, differences from other communities are an earthly demonstration of what was sent down, revealed, or discovered of the heavenly model of the multiple Books.[11]

Regarding this relationship of earthly and heavenly expressions of the Debt, Seyyed Hossein Nasr says:

> Religion in its earthly manifestation comes from the wedding between a divine Norm and a human collectivity destined providentially to receive the imprint of that Norm. From this wedding is born religion as seen in this world among different peoples and cultures. The differences in the recipient are certainly important and constitute one of the causes for the multiplicity of religious forms and phenomena, but religion itself cannot be reduced to its terrestrial embodiment.[12]

We can choose neither our place nor our time. We are created and everything we have has been given to us. By receiving this gift, we have taken on a Debt to the Creator, and we will repay Him that Debt one way or another. Return is self-realization, which requires witness to the One in the many as determining the existence of each particular thing. For that return through dialogue and difference to be possible, we are required to offer full service to the Master, as we have nothing not received from Him. We must also be persons-of-peace because after difference is admitted, no dialogue is possible unless the presence of Peace is recognized and admitted in everything and all of existence. Only through admission of the primacy of Peace, to which we are bound by being-at-peace and becoming persons-of-peace, is the diversity of things and people revealed as a sign in both inner and outer worlds to facilitate our return:

> O thou self in peace, return unto thy Lord, well-pleased, well-pleasing! Enter thou among My servants! Enter thou My Paradise![13]

Given the distinction in the human self between body and Spirit, with the unlimited multiplicity of levels between them, one may talk of dialogue within the self—as it is the self which scolds itself in its unceasing vacillation between void and Peace. The self is always susceptible to evil, as no level is absolute Peace. Ascent or return is a continuous movement of self-realization with God as its end. But it always takes place in existence, which is always a partition between higher and lower levels. For only God has no other.

Dialogue is also possible with other people who are inherently different, which can include the widest range of difference. The greater the difference, the more necessary they are as participants for our attainment of knowledge or understanding of our own lack of knowledge. Relationship with them is through being-at-peace, in which the purpose of dialogue is nothing other than Peace, which is absolute knowledge. This dialogue is caused by the possibilities it offers as an approach to Peace rather than by the other as the locus in which insurmountable difference is revealed. Recognizing this difference, the participant in dialogue recognizes the boundary, for difference is where there is a boundary. With this, human being recognizes the infinite nature of the return to the One. If we deny Him, we close off the infinite possibility of ascent, which is to deny that there is no god but God.

18. Finding Fault with Others and the Self

We always have the choice of right or wrong, good or evil, beauty or ugliness, and so on *ad infinitum*. This possibility is part of our nature as beings with free will. Given that our knowledge is limited, we cannot make final judgment regarding any of our choices. Whatever we do becomes part of our knowledge, but with some difference or conditioned in some way. God says of this:

> Yet it may happen that you will hate a thing which is better for you; and it may happen that you will love a thing which is worse for you; God knows and you know not.[1]

Although we are always unsure in judging between good and evil, we are nonetheless capable of moving toward the good and away from evil. The inexhaustibility of our capacity to choose the higher and not the lower, the beautiful and not the ugly, good and not evil, peace and not violence, and so forth, raises the question of the fullness of this capacity: Is anything truly acceptable to us except return?

Our original covenant with God makes us essentially beings of good. In essence, we are good. Self-realization means recalling that essence, revealing it, and being what it is. Thus, coming to know ourselves is coming to know good. Because God is good, our coming to know what we are and being what we know means recognizing and admitting our totality as a Debt received from God, and so returning it to Him whole and seeing the Truth of all things. Opposition to that which human being originally and finally is, consequently, means exposing ourselves to judgment and the punishment of Truth by denying it and taking the signs without accepting their revelation of Truth. Our highest capacity is in ourselves alone. Everything outside the self is a world full of signs through which we should be admonished and called to the discovery of our selves. This is so because our being derives dignity from being the image of the Ever-merciful. Denial of our authentic dignity is denial of God. For our failings, we can blame the world and the other in it or ourselves. The first approach is satanic, the other prophetic. On the first approach, we find fault with other people and the world as a whole but not with ourselves. Shortcomings are in others, and finding fault with them is a way of confirming the sense-of-self or rising above the other. Shortcomings in the self entail accepting signs in the world or the self without recognizing their reference to Unity. This is forgetting as the contrary to remembrance. Everything created becomes damned after it loses its nature as a sign and memento of the Creator.

In our material existence, we test our theories through action. Thereby we perceive, take, change, and build. The states of our self imprint themselves on the world. But God calls us to turn our gaze to the heavens and to understand how there is no disharmony in their creation. However long we look, we will find nothing but perfection. Our gaze will return to us tired and confused.[2] The external world is perfectly made, but we experience tension in contact with the world. That experience may present as imperfection of the one or the other or of both. The tension between the self and the world is normally interpreted so that we take ourselves for unquestioned measure and the world for incomplete object of our knowledge and action. Out of such an understanding of the self, the need arises to remove the faults in the world so as to resolve the tension at the boundary. This is the human condition after the fall or the loss of our original nakedness toward the world and the world's nakedness toward us.

The world was created perfect. So were we, but, as beings with free will, we have the ability to be creators. In this lies the riddle of our loss of original perfection. God is, to be sure, the only Creator. He asks us: "Is there any creator, apart from God?"[3] and again "So blessed be God, the fairest of creators!"[4] and "And God created you and what you make."[5]

Whenever we undertake "creation," as a being whose character has been realized by the beautiful divine names, our will may be in harmony with God's or opposed to it. Any act of ours which arises from such harmony is sacred. We may express ourselves in virtue and art, in holy living. When our act does not arise from such harmony, then we experience ourselves as Creator. We place ourselves at the heart of all existence. Virtue and art require rational interpretation. Then historians and philosophers are required to try to find connections between and bring into agreement the mysterious link of art and quality, on the one hand, and the new acceptance of the decisiveness and superiority of human reason, on the other.[6]

According to God's statement in the Recitation, Iblis was the first to form such an accusation of the other and take himself as the measure of the relationship to the world and to God. He says to God, "Now, for Thy perverting me, I shall surely sit in ambush for them on Thy upright path."[7]

The second response is prophetic. Here, human being blames itself for mistakes and sin, as did the Prophet Adam and his wife Eve, after they transgressed the prohibition: "We have wronged ourselves!"[8]

With this admission, we confirm our ability to discover knowledge in ourselves and to be what we know. This ability comes from the condition of having fallen. In the beginning, we had a perfect world that mirrored our own self. The entire science of preserving this condition consisted of following the prohibition against approaching the sacred tree. By transgressing the prohibition, which was possible through the wrong use of free will, we came to the lowest depth or the furthest remove from God. And by accepting guilt for this condition, we opened ourselves to receiving the lesson: "Thereafter Adam received certain words from his Lord, and He turned toward him; truly He turns, and is All-merciful."[9]

The words Adam received offer us doctrine, ritual, and virtue as the means of turning from the depths toward the heights, from fall to ascent, in order to regain what we had in the beginning, which we could have kept if we had respected the prohibition.

Whenever we take the order of the external world, and particularly the social order, as the key object of our knowledge, any disagreement between us as "knowers" and that which we "know" will appear to us to be the fault of others. The world must then seem chaotic, while our own knowledge, which is the relationship of the knower to the world, appears absolute. For one in such a relationship, all that remains is to present the world as wrong and to initiate action to fix it. Then action becomes our highest capacity. Understood in this light, this is creation in an imperfect world and humanity in accordance with the knowledge of one who takes his or her image of the world for the world itself. Thus, knowledge and action have become a veil over the self that appears unproblematic to itself. Such a person submits everything, with the exception of their own self, to their own knowledge and action. They take their passions for gods, with regard to which God says:

> Hast thou seen him who has taken his caprice to be his god, and God has led him astray out of a knowledge and set a seal upon his hearing and his heart and laid a covering on his eyes?[10]

Such a condition of the self finds confirmation in the evidence of having changed the world and society and of having broken down their resistances. No form of existence that is weaker can have any value beyond submission to that which is more powerful than it. Actualizing the stronger-weaker relationship entails reducing relationships in the multiplicity of existence to their quantitative expression and the exclusion of qualities. Tolerance in principle is refraining from acting out of power, where the other and the different are weaker. It is, moreover, looking for qualitative reasons for the difference of the other.

The fight against evil in the other is the dominant content of political ideologies. In political centers, there are always those who dispose of greater power than others in their environment. Given that those at the center consider themselves the ones who know and present their knowledge as an ideology of order, they blame others for any contradictions between their picture of order and reality and wage constant war against them. And that is the satanic relationship of the self to the world. The prophetic relationship is the opposite: War against the external world is less significant and so less decisive for human being than war within the self and against its acceptance of gods other than God.

In this (prophetic) approach, God's mercy is accepted as all-encompassing. Therefore, the struggle for the self is more important than condemning others and subordinating them to the image one has, which, it is worth admitting, is always less than the self has the potential to be. That potential would be approximation to the Prophet.

Our experience of the external world is the first level of our sense-of-self. We clearly see the great remote heavens up above and earth near below. Between them are scattered all things. We are impotent in front of the world which stretches from the depths to the unreachable heights as long as we take it to be all there is and independent of our interiority. That stimulates us to seek fault in it, of which God says:

> Thou seest not in the creation of the All-merciful any imperfection. Return thy gaze; seest thou any fissure? Then return thy gaze again, and again, and thy gaze comes back to thee dazzled, weary.[11]

As long as we seek shortcomings in the external world, we presume and feel a lack in ourselves. Our action to remedy the world is transference of passions outside of ourselves so that they may be slaked there. Recognition of the perfection of the external world is the same as recognition of perfect human creaturehood, which may be revealed and realized. Of our creaturehood, God says, "It is God who made for you the earth a fixed place, and heaven for an edifice; and He shaped you, and shaped you well"[12] and "We indeed created Man in the fairest uprightness, then We restored him the lowest of the low—save those who believe, and do righteous deeds."[13] Accordingly, our original creaturehood, like our final possibility, is Beauty. It cannot be otherwise given that God is Beautiful and that He loves Beauty.[14] God created us and all that we do.[15] Whenever Beauty is not to be seen in us

or what we do, that means that we have lost Peace as the only goal in
our being-at-peace and that we have ceased to be faithful to the Faithful and beautiful to the Beautiful.
Assuming deficiency means accepting void as primary or that there
are gods other than God. Evil arrives in the world through that deficiency in human interiority or through that which is undiscovered or
unrealized in us and is our original and beautiful uprightness. That is
the sense of Satan's response to God, "Now, because you have de-
ceived me." For such a one, the external world is faulty, which means
that so is its Creator. The response of Adam and Eve is entirely different, "We have wronged ourselves!" Such a response allows the gaze
to be returned to the one who looks, in recognition of the fact that the
earth and the heavens and all between them were created perfect and
so too was human interiority, from body to Spirit, and everything in
between. By this turn from the external world to the self, this recognition of the truth in the unrevealed self, we add perfect human being
to the perfect world and bear witness to divine Unity, from Which
everything in existence is and to Which everything returns.[16]
Wherever and however the human self is, its creaturehood is perfect. Therefore, the highest possibility is return, the measure of which
is nothing other than perfect human being. The condition for this is
liberation from gods other than God. Not even perfect human being,
which is the end of human being, deserves that anyone be his or her
servant. A free human being is he who admits only God for his Master. Given that service to God is also the expression of the original
and highest capacity of everything in existence, the free human being
accepts them in their dignity. There is nothing that in the ultimate significance of its existence is not God's servant.[17] Only in the fullness
of service to the Master do we realize His beautiful names in our nature. Our relationship to everything in the world is relationship to
God:

> It belongs not to any mortal that God should give him the Book,
> the Judgment, the Prophethood, then he should say to men, "Be
> you servants to me apart from God." Rather, "Be you masters
> in that you know the Book, and in that you study."[18]

19. FREE WILL AND THE COVENANT

Our encounter with God is different from the relations of all other things in existence with their Creator, both jointly and individually, on the one hand, and with the Transcendental, on the other. As creatures, we are at both the very end of everything that is in existence and the very beginning. We gather in ourselves all the names that were at the beginning of creation in the One and that are at the end of creation dispersed in the particularity of each existent. By being at the end, we gather in ourselves all this diversity. With all our potential, we are between the end of existence and its beginning. We thus include everything between void and the Real.

All the worlds are God's discourse of Himself. They are interconnected so that some reveal others in ascending or descending relation. Humanity gathers in itself that which is dispersed over the worlds. The Book sent down by God to the human heart is God's discourse of Himself, but it is also a call to us to recognize the signs of this discourse in the external world and in ourselves.

God offers us confidence. We can refuse or accept the offer. The offer itself includes God's restriction of His own absolute power. Voluntary acceptance of the offer determines our innermost essence and is that which makes the relationship of human being and God different from all other forms of existence. Our free will, which allows us to accept, but also to reject what is offered, is God's voluntary self-limitation, or, in other words, His confirmation of the Absolute that is manifest in His being the All-merciful, the Ever-merciful. God gives us freedom and trusts us to use the gift to return to the One. Thus, in the relation of confidence, there are two wills at play—human and divine.

Humanity has accepted that freedom and so, in the face of any decision, we find ourselves constantly between two possibilities—volition or involuntariness. This possibility constantly distances us from God or brings us toward Him. Doing good brings us forward, sin distances us. Our potential lies not in the fullness of knowledge; rather, we are beings of final or first possibilities, but never just that. We are in a dilemma with regard to the offered or given word. We are indebted by our creaturehood. We have nothing which the Creator has not given us. But our confidence in and with God makes the recipient responsible for the received. That is our debt toward the Creator. We dispose of it on the basis of free will, which is another thing we have received. It shapes our humanity, the fundamental sign of which is Adam, the first human being and the first prophet of God. In him, both extremes of humanity were revealed, the highest and the lowest.

Adam is the end or the gathering of all creation. Everything that is distinguished in the external world, from the highest heavens to the earth and all between them, is gathered in us, from the Spirit which God breathed into us to the body formed of earth by His two hands and everything between them. Humanity is, thus, at the end or the bottom of creation, but with the potential to encompass and transcend all of existence. God's intention to create the world includes us. The return of everything to God is our return. Our relationship to God with all our possibilities, including free will, is a complete contract, to which both we and God swear fidelity. This contract between God and humanity determines the position of Adam: "And We made covenant with Adam before, but he forgot, and We found in him no constancy."[1]

Our original placement at the heart of all creation meant that we saw in everything external the same as was in us and in ourselves the same as was in all the world. This position at the heart of all creation could not in any way usurp the primary centrality of Unity, which is manifest in everything, but it can never be equated with that in which it is manifest. That is the meaning of Gabriel's demand for belief in angels, who are, in fact, God's messengers. They endow each sign with meaning in their discourse of the Creator. Thus, the world and human being and the book were sent down from God so that they might all return to Him.

Human perfection, located at the center of creation, does not annihilate the whole of either the world or of human being. The world as a whole consists of the countless levels of being separating Unity from void. So too it is with us. The world and human being are two, but each reflects the other. They are separate but linked. In this way, they reveal their derivation from another world and so the possibility of unhindered ascent toward the Intellect as the first revelation of Unity.

This centrality in creation, which reveals the infinite nearness and remoteness of Unity, is guaranteed by the contract of the forbidden tree:

> And We said, "Adam, dwell thou, and thy wife, in the Garden, and eat thereof easefully where you desire; but draw not nigh this tree, lest you be evildoers." Then Satan caused them to slip there from and brought them out of that they were in.[2]

The tree that God showed to Adam is the limit of free will and so the measure of bearing with or violating confidence. Our "I" and all the external world, with a clear boundary between them, testify to the One and that there is no real but Him. That they are free means that there are two possibilities in every choice—one which turns toward God or the forbidden nature of the tree and the other which turns from Him, which is satanic and encourages them to transgress the order and descend toward void.

When Adam transgressed God's order, reaching for the fruit of the forbidden tree, wanting thus to deny the boundary which reveals the duality of the world, his fall to the bottom of existence took place. God's confidence that human being could support the limitation and our confidence in the meaning of it maintained Unity in all multiplicity. For human being, all things are and have been signs of the One.

Through the fall, we did not lose our original nature. Forgetting is only the covering over of our original uncoveredness. Transgression of the boundary revealed nakedness to Adam and his wife Eve, and they began to cover themselves.[3] Covering, of which reaching for the leaf of paradise informs us, testifies to the new condition which arose through forgetting of the covenant with God. But his regret or turn to the One allowed him to renew the covenant. He was at the bottom of the Valley of Tears, but God sent down to him the Cube, as a sign of the renewal of consciousness of limit and measure and of righteousness restored:

> God has appointed the Ka'ba, the Holy House as an establishment for men, and the holy month, the offering, and the necklaces—that you may know that God knows all that is in the heavens and all that is in the earth, and that God has knowledge of everything.[4]

All the signs on the horizon, on earth, in heaven, and in between preserved their clarity after the fall. Only our interiority became clouded. From the Valley of existence, in which the original condition was transformed by transgression of the prohibition, renewal is possible. But it is a return for which doctrine, ritual, and virtue are required.

Fallen humanity has the Ka'ba as the beginning of return to the original covenant with God and the discovery of that which is hidden in forgetting, as God says, "From whatsoever place thou issuest, turn thy face to the Sacred Mosque."[5] So, we have turned toward our highest possibility, the Praised as Most Beautiful Model. The cardinal sign of our return is the Ascension of the Praised, whereby in one night, which is to say in the world of fallen human being, he realized the return from the Sacred to the Furthest Mosque, from the world of form to Primordial Intellect:

> Glory be to Him, who carried His servant by night from the Sacred Mosque to the Furthest Mosque the precincts of which We have blessed, that We might show him some of Our signs. He is the All-hearing, the All-seeing.[6]

That is our highest possibility: to discover and confess the inviolability of the boundary between the world and the self and, by confessing the boundary, to direct all our praise to God, Lord of the worlds, the All-merciful, the Ever-merciful, the King of the Day of Debt.

The word, which human being gave in establishing the covenant of confidence with God, we ceaselessly betray, as forgetfulness makes us unreliable in the keeping of promises or responses in the heart of our being:

> And when thy Lord took from the Children of Adam, from their loins, their seed, and made them testify touching themselves, "Am I not your Lord?" They said, "Yes, we testify"—lest you should say on the Day of Resurrection, "As for us, we were heedless of this," or lest you say, "Our fathers were idolaters aforetime, and we were seed after them. What, wilt Thou then destroy us for deeds of the vain-doers?"[7]

The covenant with Adam includes all his posterity. But, he realized himself between forgetting, which is never such that it entirely destroys the covenant, and remembrance, whereby human being can be raised up from the lowest depth to the highest height. At any point between these two extremes, forgetting threatens us with the possibility that we will introduce gods other than God into the heart of our covenant with God. These gods may be passions, imaginings, fears, plans, or any other finite thing.

All the prophets renew the original covenant with God, expelling from the center everything other than God, overturning all iconic or graven images, so that to everything they might allocate the properties of sign and of Unity, which becomes one-and-only in the sacred and inviolate center. That is God's word of covenant—that we associate nothing and no one with God. It has been renewed by Noah and Abraham, Moses and David, John and Jesus. From this renewal come the revealed books and the peoples they inform. The revealed books are restitution of the overturned boundary: They issue from the One into the most profound core of pure humanity, and thence into discourse and the world, so that they might dwell within them both within the boundary and beyond. This is the reason why the covenant encompasses all the People of the Book.[8] Although the covenant may become a part of speech in time, even those whose senses of self are formed by it may betray it.

But God will not betray His word, "And We gave Moses the Book; and there was difference regarding it, and but for a word that preceded from thy Lord, it had been decided between them; and they are in doubt of it disquieting."[9] Given our position as a being who has received freedom, our finite will has doubt for its shadow. For as long as our will runs up against the limit set down for it by the self-restraint of absolute Will, then it must be doubtful. Only by comparison of that will with the Will can we eradicate that doubt. That doubt partakes of the nature of our limited knowledge. Where doubt is, fear is, too. Both the one and the other may be dissipated only by knowledge.

Our openness toward the fullness of coming-to-know allows us ceaselessly to change as a knower who, through knowing, comes to be closer to the Known, who knows everything. Only in covenant with God is the irreducibility of difference acceptable and bearable. Every sense-of-self is related to a "Thou" on the basis of a little knowledge. It may never know the other as it knows itself and may never know itself as God does. Therefore, God's witness of the relationship of the self and a "Thou" is the only guarantee of their capacity to ascend, with the recognition of all the limits and so of their differences. This ascent from the depths toward the most beautiful righteousness is not possible without acceptance of the need to suffer/tolerate differences. Difference there always is, given the word which informs the covenant of human being and God, compared to the word given by human being.

This difference with regard to the Word places each of us in an unrepeatable position that is ours alone, with regard to God, Who believes in us, and so with regard to the Debt we have to the Creator. For He has limited His will so that we might come to Him of our own will:

Had thy Lord willed, He would have made mankind
one nation; but they continue in their differences.[10]

Afterword: The Text and Its Power

Every human question unfolds in the world and language. If we accept that the world is an expression and revelation of the One, then we should accept that different languages can show the One in the many and the many in the One. Divine speech cannot be limited by language. That is why Revelation is in principle possible in every language: so that every human individual and group partakes of the dignity of origin and return. According to traditional wisdom, God is the Creator of both humanity and what we do. From this, it follows that He created the different languages. They too are, accordingly, signs, both as wholes and in their various parts.

Revelations are available in a given tongue, whether as oral or textual transmission. But, access to them is possible from any language, as their discourse may in principle be translated so that the semantic essence is not betrayed. The following verse suggests this clearly:

> We have sent no Messenger save with the tongue of his people,
> that he might make all clear to them.[1]

The variety of human languages and the presence of revelation as text in only some of them cannot mean that some individuals or peoples are deprived of their right to individual and collective dignity.[2]

Language allows both world and human being, as two images of one and the same God, to be clarified. The variety of languages does not limit or condition this clarity.

The author's intention has been to show that grounds exist in the fundamental texts of the muslim tradition to support toleration of the other and the different. This does not relate to toleration only. Given that recognition of right in everything and human perfection are the goals of this teaching and that doctrine, tradition, and virtue are just means to these goals, the presence of the other and the different and the approach to them may in principle be explained as the condition of human self-realization.

The reason for writing this book is to oppose the prevailing opinion that intolerance is inherent to the Islamic textual heritage as a whole. When a muslim takes up either tolerance or intolerance as attitudes to the other, they are determined by the historical conditions in which the sense-of-self was formed. Investigation into what is affirmed to be an individual's or society's reality at a given time requires that one determine the best model of individual and collective self-hood. This best model is contained in the reasons for creation, for the sending of God's prophets, and for the revelation of His books. Insofar as an individual's human nature comes to realization through the most beautiful divine names and attributes, which is the purpose of all sacred doctrine, ritual, and virtue, then one may say that the muslim relation to the world and everything in it is tolerant or intolerant in the best way possible.

It is worth repeating that muslims are a community or people bound, above all, by acceptance of the Recitation. One may say of them that they are the People of the Recitation. But the Book has been present to individuals in different languages and at the different times at which this people has been active. We find ourselves always between two final possibilities—witness to Unity and His denial through the association of gods with God. We are originally open toward the Absolute. Whenever that openness is threatened, our sense-of-self is covered, and we are coverers. When such covering is taken for a final value, it becomes association of gods with God or idolatry.

For us to bear witness to Unity, we must have the Book. But, even given the Book we may be coverers or idolaters. Understanding the differences between these two, real being with the Book and dissimulation, allows us to see how virtue and universal justice are the criteria of being what we say we are.

If such a reading of the text does confirm the possibility of grounding tolerance, one unresolved issue remains: Where does this other reading come from on which the advocates of intolerance call? They are readings of the self-same text, but two entirely different views of it. Different readers find in the text the justification for entirely contrary positions and behavior. One group explains and confirms its position of tolerance; the other, its position of intolerance toward others and the different.

It is hardly controversial that the muslim holy texts advocate, enjoin, and enable human dignity alongside the various other doctrinal paths to the self-same God, all of which enjoin their adherents to virtue. What is controversial is that these same texts should be taken and interpreted to incite and justify denial of the dignity of and violence against the other.

Tolerance and intolerance are always relations between people. Whether we tolerate or fail to tolerate the other or different, our sense-of-self stands always between the best and worst we are capable of. The same is true of those who are or are not tolerated. Neither the one nor the other has an unchanging or inalterable sense-of-self. If Peace is the desired goal of this relationship, attaining Him presupposes that the possibility of change be recognized on both sides. When the muslim is the one who does or does not tolerate the other or different, it is to be desired that the sense-of-self change after the sublime model. That model is contained in the highest meaning of the holy texts and the most beautiful nature of the prophet the Praised. It is only in reference to that sublime model that one can determine deficiencies of knowledge, opinion, and behavior that manifest as insults to human dignity. Such determination is necessary because human being is a dependent being, and there is always the possibility that we might be better than we are and that we might steadily climb the ladder of being to find our authentic and most beautiful potential.

While the text of the Recitation may be unalterable in its written form, the same does not go for any given interpretation. The one and the same text is available to all. It is God's discourse, as are existence as a whole and human being. They are always expressions of the All-merciful, the Ever-merciful. Inwardly, they are one and the same. But no reading of the holy text can be the same or final, given that every individual is an inimitable and unique original, always in between possibilities—the worst and the most beautiful. The reading is determined by the totality of sense-of-self, which is in constant change. Thus the question is raised: can the relationship of the reader and the text help change the human tendency toward evil?

If the answer to this question is negative, the undertaking which gave rise to this book is bereft of meaning.

No conclusions can be drawn from the text of the Recitation itself with regard to the justification of violence against others. If one tries to, one commits violence against the text. This does not mean that human being is right to tolerate violence, but doing violence and tolerating it are not the same, any more than evil and good. They are not because the dignity of human being, of the world, and of the Book are all guaranteed by God, Whom they reveal as His images. They may be measured only in terms of the highest goal—return to God and passage through the judgment, when sentence will be based on a just weighing of every atom of good done and every atom of evil done.

The holy text is available to the reader as it is. We cannot change it. But, the reading subject can and does encounter and read it. Every reading is determined by the text and the subject's sense-of-self. The holy text as read and the sense-of-self of the reader provide the interpretation. The text is inalterable, but the sense-of-self is not. It is alterable in two directions, toward the good and the bad. It is always a mix of the two, but change toward the good is change toward realization or its higher potential.

Interpretation is also subject to change, which means that the sense-of-self changes with regard to the text. Every reader gains something from the text read. This means that what he or she brings to the reading—a sense-of-self torn between a tendency to evil, overcoming of it, and return to Peace—shifts from a lower to a higher condition. This re-forming of the sense-of-self from a lower to a higher level is a possibility of the sacred text as a whole. Grasping the holy text to serve a sense-of-self confirmed in its own darkness does not reflect closure of the text per se. It is closure of the self.

> We have to accept that the morality of the Qur'an goes beyond the morality of its interpreters. In many ways, the text of the Qur'an set the moral courses which interpreting communities from the past could not appropriately understand. In some ages, interpreters of tradition have totally overlooked the moral essence of the epistles of the Qur'an and produced features that closed the Qur'an in myopic and inappropriate views. . . . As Muslims, we stand next to a religious belief that morality of the Qur'an shall always exceed the morality of its interpreters. In other words, I do not believe that human beings can have a claim upon the fact that they have understood the message of the Qur'an perfectly and entirely. Inaccessibleness of the Qur'an's moral message is inevitable, but that is also a stimulus for it to join the everlasting dynamic of moral exploring and interpreting.[3]

The text of the Recitation is God's message to all people. According to that Message, it is born out of mercy for the world. As such, its meaning lies in addressing, stimulating, and leading people to the common good. When interpretations are such that they incite violence and may be used to justify it, this darkens and denies the general advocacy of human dignity which is at the heart of the Message. When people in today's world connect the idea of *islam* with images of brutality, suffering, oppression, and violence, islam becomes the name for an ideology that annihilates all that is opposed to those images. If *islam* authentically understood is the relationship of the human being in search of peace (the *muslim*) to God, Who is Peace (*al-Salām*), then the understanding and practice of islam held by human beings is something quite different from the *islam* of the holy text.

One might say here that there are two different and mutually opposed phenomena denoted by one and the same name. Distinguishing them is a very hard and convoluted undertaking. Both these phenomena, finally considered, are different interpretations of one and the same text. These interpretations arise from different formations of the subjects approaching the text. These subjects are formed in different interpretative communities. The subject approaching interpretation introduces a sense-of-self so formed that it wants to confirm itself in the text. The text itself, in its inalterability and in the abundance it offers, plays the role of changing the sense-of-self to accord with its own sublime possibilities.

The ideological distortion of Islam is an exceptional and unacceptable phenomenon. This is because today almost all muslim countries are ruled by authoritarian regimes that disable serious discussion of political, cultural, and economic issues. Moreover, muslims today are among the most powerless, most controlled, and most humiliated people on the planet. Islam as an ideology provides them no way out of that condition. The idea of Ideology should be understood as a term for the human undertaking to reduce existence to the measurable world and its quantitative expression and our conviction that we possess everything required to be an independent reformer and governor of the world. Through this reduction of humanity to one level of existence, instrumental reason is adopted as sufficient means for humanity to determine and attain our final goal on earth. But *islam* is a relationship of human being and God as a covenant in which two wills participate.

With *islam* as the clear relationship between human being and our sublime model, muslims can share the same hope that inspires every human being in the quest for dignity of life. Moreover, as seekers for total Peace, those who grow morally though witness can contribute to the realization of humanity more generally. What so-called Muslims today confess very often lacks moral grounding and, consequently, moral responsibility. There is no greater loss than to lose one's moral

grounding. That is the meaning of all resistance to any simple blind
response to violence and injustice:

> O you who have attained to faith!
> Be ever steadfast in your devotion to God,
> bearing witness to the truth in all equity,
> and never let hatred of anyone lead you
> into the sin of deviating from justice.
> Be just: this is closest to being conscious.
> And remain conscious of God: verily,
> God is aware of all that you do.[4]

Notes

1. Translator's note: Because it is the author's intention in this book to
argue against reified forms of tradition, particularly in the understanding of
religion and religious values, I have followed his usage in Bosnian of writing identifiers (terms that identify one as belonging to a particular tradition—muslim, christian, jewish, hindu, and so on) without capitalization
when they refer to the living tradition of thought, belief, and ritual of a community of self-critical and aware believers who seek self-realization in relation to the eternal values revealed by God through that tradition. The author
considers them to make up the core group of the faithful of all the world
religions and to have more in common with each other than they do with
their nominal co-religionists. He refers to them as the "Nation of the Just."
They follow the road to responsible autonomy, which comes with the understanding of tradition. When the terms are capitalized, the reference is to
the reified traditions of ideological identification, whereby aspects of the
tradition are deployed in ways that harden the boundaries between self and
other and between in and out groups so that the unrealized self submits to
the tyranny of partial values or of symbols and signs mistaken for that
which they intimate; thus these traditions are constituted as idols, insulated
from critical reflection or the action of sympathy, compassion, or mercy.
The result is normally either a condition of heteronomy (simple and rigid
submission) or of irresponsible and disguised autonomy (misrecognition of
one's own will as that of God or the dictate of tradition). Thus, the *muslim*
is the person-of-peace, whose life is dedicated to finding peace for him- or
herself and for others and so to being-at-peace, or *islam*; while the *Muslim*

is one who has built his personal and group identity around the ritual symbols of a reified *Islam*, while ignoring or being ignorant of the fact that their only value is as signposts on the path to being-at-peace.

2. Translator's note: The author uses a term throughout the essay that has no exact equivalent in English. This is *Jastvo*, the root of which is the pronoun *Ja*, which means "I." It may refer to the principle of individuation; the individuated self; the sense that the self has of being individuated; and, finally, subjectivity. It will therefore be translated as "self," "sense-of-self," and "subject," as the context requires.

3. Translator's note: The use of capitalization of pronouns or abstract nouns in this text nearly always refers to God or one of His aspects or attributes. Thus, for example, the self refers to selfhood as it is manifest in human being, but the Self refers to God as the Principle and Source of all Selfhood.

4. Translator's note: The author has requested that the translation be as gender neutral as possible. This problem and the difficulties it poses for English are well known. The translator apologizes for any resulting inelegancy of language or construction.

1. I, Thou, and He

1. The virtue of tolerance gained prominence on the world stage during the rise of enlightenment thought in the seventeenth and eighteenth centuries. Dictionary treatment of the concept normally goes as follows: cf. Engl. *tolerance* (lat. *tolerantia*, from *tolerare* [to endure]), to bear: acceptance (endurance, suffering), particularly of the opinions, beliefs, and behavior of others; freedom from bigotry, narrow-mindedness, or prejudice; Engl. *toleration* (lat. *toleratio* [*-onis*], from *tolerare*): particularly freedom to hold religious views that differ from established views. The *Act of Toleration* is an English legal document from 1689, whereby conditional upon an oath of allegiance and disavowal of the doctrine of transubstantiation, Protestant dissenters from the Church of England were relieved of restrictions previously placed upon them regarding the free conduct of their religion in accordance with its rules. Toleration, it should be stressed, is inseparable from the divide that marks the relationship between the traditional and the modern. As the end of the second Christian millennium approached, increasingly complex and tense relations among global factions imposed the question of tolerance in its various forms. Some of the more important literature on the subject includes: Gopin, *Between Eden and Armageddon: The Future of World Religions, Violence and Peacemaking*; Heyd, *Toleration: An Elusive Virtue*; Kamen, *The Rise of Toleration*; Katz, *Exclusiveness and Tolerance*; Larsen, *Religious Toleration: The Variety of Rites from Cyrus to DeFoe*; Mendus, *Justifying Toleration: Conceptual and Historical Perspectives*; Mendus, *Toleration and the Limits of Liberalism*; Remer, *Humanism*

and the Rhetoric of Toleration; Sachedina, *Islamic Roots of Democratic Pluralism*; Seligman, *Modest Claim: Dialogues and Essays on Tolerance and Tradition*; and Walzer, *On Toleration.* On the other, otherness, and tolerance/toleration from perspectives that may be considered either islamic or historically related to Islam/Muslims, see: Friedmann, *Tolerance and Coercion in Islam: Interfaith Relations in the Muslim Tradition*; Khan, *Human Rights in the Muslim World: Fundamentalism, Constitutionalism, and International Politics*; Sadri and Sadri, *Reason, Freedom, and Democracy in Islam: Essential Writings of 'Abdolkarim Soroush*; and Said and Sharify-Funk, *Cultural Diversity and Islam.*

2. Translator's note: As the text itself makes clear, an important part of the author's intention in this work is to counter the interpretation of *islam* as based on submission, obedience, lack of personal will, and therefore failure to achieve autonomy. He presents the traditional (and Kantian) point-of-view that autonomy lies in harmonization of the self and the will with universal values, as represented by the divine names, rather than in "pure" self-determination, which is effectively just the misrecognition of heteronomy (which is close to what the author means by "association unto God" or idolatry, taking a contingent for an ultimate value). As the text and the following author's note make clear, the author stresses the etymological links between the cluster of terms *islam-muslim-salam* as a way of focusing attention on peace as the heart of *islam*. Being-at-peace (*islam*) is an integral part of the Debt (*din*), the three other dimensions of which are faith (*iman*), doing what is good and beautiful (*ihsan*), and knowledge of the hour (*sa'a*). It is important to realize that *islam* is "the peace of God that passeth all understanding," rather than an imposition of homogeneity. It comprehends difference rather than excluding it. The author's strategy of translation is intended to preserve key semantic linkages that exist in the Recitation and to avoid any form of reification of *islam*, as it is most common in modern ideological approaches to this sacred tradition. He does this by using translations that are all based on the root of the Bosnian word for peace, *mir*. We have accordingly translated the relevant Bosnian terms as person-of-peace (*muslim, miritelj*), being-at-peace (*islam, mirenje*), and Peace (*al-Salām, Mir*). On this issue, see more in Mahmutćehajić, "Fundamentalism versus Traditional Intellectuality." For further explanation of why the term *din* has been translated as Debt, see Chapter 3, note 3.

3. These three terms derive from the same Arabic verbal root *slm*; *islam* is the fourth form from the infinitive of the root; *muslim* is the fourth form active participle; *salam* is the verbal noun of the verb *salima*. These concepts cover very wide semantic ranges. In translating them, we have respected the connection between them, which is often lost, particularly in ideological interpretation and use of the text.

4. The use of the term "being-at-peace" (*islam*) may, in line with contemporary usage, suggest two contradictory meanings. First, there are the

various things that "religious nationalism" uses it to mean. Secondly, there is the meaning ascribed by traditional intellectuals. One might say that our endeavor is essentially an attempt to question and to bring into question the first set of meanings through interpretation and affirmation of the second set. "Being-at-peace" is transcendence of all religious form and encounter with the Truth. The concept, therefore, meets the need for exoteric exclusion at the same time as it maintains an esoteric claim to general inclusiveness. In its second meaning, "being-at-peace" is both the exoteric framework of a particular religion and the esoteric core of all religions, transcending all individual forms.

5. The crucial importance of the terms "Self" (*Jastvo*) and "Thou-hood" (*Tistvo*) for our discussion should be stressed. Although used here principally with the meanings they have for the Judaic, Christian, and Islamic traditions, these ideas belong to all forms of *sophia perennis*. Differences in the forms taken by the various traditions may be reflected in how Self and Thou-hood are stressed. Both may depend on the expression of the Utmost Reality, the Essential that reveals itself in everything else. This introduces a third person, He, who is always implicit in the I-Thou relationship, whether as God or as the worlds of existence and the beings that inhabit them. The Self (*Ātmā*) is He, as it is "fully objective" insofar as it excludes individuation, while He (*Hūwa*) is Self and therefore "fully subjective" insofar as it excludes all reification. The Sufi formula *Lā anā wa lā anta: Hūwa* ("Not I nor Thou, but He") corresponds, therefore, to the expression from the Upanishads *Tat Tvam Asi* ("That Thou Art"), cf. Schuon, *Spiritual Perspectives and Human Facts*, 102.

6. See Preface, translator's note 1, on the distinction between *muslim* and *Muslim*.

7. The Arabic term *din* is commonly translated as "religion," but its basic meaning is "debt" or "bond" and so our obligation toward God arising from our relationship of creaturehood and our transgression in the Garden. See note 3 in Chapter 3 for further discussion and references.

2. THE ONE AND THE MANY

1. Given that this essay is written from a traditional point-of-view, most quotations are taken from the *Qur'an* (the Recitation), the Torah, the Psalms, the Gospels, and related texts. Quotations are from Arberry, *The Koran Interpreted* and *The Thompson Chain-Reference Bible: King James Version*. The *Qur'anic* quotations have been modified to reflect the author's preferred translation of key terms and preserve semantic links otherwise lost. This relates particularly to the translation of the key terms: *din, muslim, islam,* and *al-Salām,* as respectively the Debt, person-of-peace, being-at-peace, and Peace. Citation of and references to the Recitation (*Qur'an*) will be given by chapter number (*sura*) and verse (*ayat*). "Associating anything with God" (*shirk*) is the other or negative side of "witness to Unity"

(*tawḥīd*). Witness to Unity is a condition of being a person-of-peace (*muslim*). This witness is an important content of all prophecy (*Qur'an* 21:25): "And We never sent a Messenger before thee, except that We revealed to him, saying: 'There is no god but I; so serve Me.'" Associating anything with God, according to the divine message in the Recitation, is the only unforgivable sin (4:48): "God forgives not that aught should be with Him associated, less than that He forgives to whomsoever He will." Witness to the Unity of God is our deepest and unchanging nature. Denial of this or associating anything other than Him with God is the annihilation or betrayal of humanity. Associating something other than Him with God or denying His Unity may take various forms, ranging from willfulness and fancies to beings, systems, and idols. The worst form, however, of association is following one's own whims, as God himself says (28:50): "Who is further astray than he who follows his caprice, without guidance from God?"; and (25:43): "Hast thou seen him who has taken his caprice to be his god?" When the passions are taken for God, they are invisible and can be covered up by external behavior that is in total contradiction to the individual's internal state. One way to deny the One is to claim that God is knowable. For, "like him there is naught" (42:11). His essence cannot be determined. Cleaving fast to the knowledge of His unknowability is wisdom. Only through this can one learn to know His attributes and acts or recognize the signs in the world or the self.

2. *Qur'an* 4:48.

3. Ibid. 51:49.

4. Ibid. 2:186.

5. Ibid. 2:152.

6. Ibid. 50:16.

7. Ibid. 112:4.

8. Ibid. 42:11.

9. Human freedom, according to the Recitation, is realizable only through witness to Unity (*tawḥīd*). Everything other than God which a human being serves or becomes beholden to is associated with Him, which is the contrary to or opposite of witness to Unity and so an unforgivable sin. Only through witness to Unity may service to anything other than God be refused, as God commands in the Recitation (6:19): "Say, He is only one God and I am quit of that you associate." According to al-Qāshāni, freedom is "the release from enslavement to others." "There are," this writer says, "three degrees of freedom. First, there is being freed from enslavement to carnal desires. Second, there is special freedom—from enslavement to aspirations, through the obliteration of the personal will within the will of Truth. Finally, there is the most special freedom of all—from enslavement to custom and tradition, through their effacement in the revelation of the Light of Lights." (Qāshāni, *A Glossary of Sufi Technical Terms*, 27).

10. See Bukhari, 9:482.

11. *Qur'an* 39:53–55.

12. Ibid. 37:96.

13. See ibid. 3:55.

14. *Qur'an* 10:109. It is worth stressing here the place of debt in the order of being. The totality of existence reveals God; human being is the core of all existence; consciousness of the debt to God is the core of human being; connection with God (alliance, prayer) is the core of consciousness of debt; commemoration or appeal to God is the core of connection with Him.

15. "The Opening" is the translation of the Arabic *Sūrah al-Fātihah.* This surah is also called *Fātihat al-Kitāb* ("The Opening of the Book"), *Umm al-Kitāb* ("The Mother of the Book"), *Sūrat al-Hamd* ("The Image of Praise"), and *Asās al-Qur'ān* ("The Foundation of the Recitation"). It is mentioned in the Recitation as *As-Sab' al-Mathani* ("The Sevenfold Repetition"), as it is repeated at every station of the five obligatory daily prayers.

16. After Chittick, *The Sufi Path of Knowledge: Ibn al-'Arabi's Metaphysics of Imagination*, 103.

17. *Qur'an* 16:125.

3. THE STRANGER

1. *Qur'an* 6:103.

2. Ibid. 14:4.

3. Ar. *al-din al-qayyim* ("the standing debt"). See *Qur'an* 9:36, 12:40, 30:30. It is worth noting that *din al qayyim* is semantically connected to the "upright path," "the most beautiful uprightness," and the divine name, "the Standing." In the original of this text, as in many others, the author has translated the Arabic term *din* into Bosnian as *dug*, which may be rendered in English as "debt," "obligation," or "bond." While it is easy to defend this decision on etymological and semantic grounds, most readers will find it somewhat unusual. There is a bias toward translation of the term as *religion*, which, although justifiable in terms of its etymological roots ("to bind"), the author considers problematic because of the connotations of reified practice and institutions accrued over time and which are not present in the original semantic context. Difficulties related to translation of the original term *din* have long been recognized, but no solution has been offered that would allow this key term from the *Qur'an* to be translated consistently in the various parts of the holy text. The solution offered here would seem to offer advantages over other suggestions made to date. For the difficulties related to translation of the term *din*, see Izutsu, *God and Man in the Qur'an: Semantics of the Qur'anic Weltanschauung*, 219–29; and Smith, *The Meaning and the End of Religion*, 287–89. Reviewing the various possibilities offered by Arabic as a language, Izutsu suggests the English term

"requital" as the most promising solution. This suggestion is very close to that adopted here. In the same discussion, Izutsu notes the link between the concepts of slavery or bondage (ar. *ibada*) and *din*. Careful consideration of this link confirms the justification for translating it with the Bosnian term *dug*, which as noted above means "debt" or "bond."
4. See *Qur'an* 4:79, 7:158, 21:107.
5. The Prophet says, "People, know that your Lord is one, your forefather one. Know that the Arab has no advantage over the stranger, nor the stranger over the Arab, nor the red over the black, nor the black over the red, except with regard to conscience." In that same statement, the Prophet also said, "Truly God has made you inviolable in your blood, your property, and your honor, just as this day, this month, and this town are inviolable" (Ibn Hanbal, *al-Musnad*, tradition 22391).
6. *Qur'an* 26:198–99.
7. See ibid. 2:216.
8. See ibid. 45:23.
9. Ibid. 29:46.
10. Muslim, 4:1409; Bukhari, 9:369–70.
11. Bukhari, 3:107–8.
12. *Qur'an* 49:13.
13. Ibid. 5:48.

4. SELF-KNOWLEDGE

1. *Qur'an* 5:69.
2. "The Lotus of the furthest boundary" (*sidrat al-muntaha*) is mentioned in the Recitation (53:13–18): "Indeed, he saw him another time by the Lote-Tree of the Boundary nigh which is the Garden of the Refuge, when there covered the Lote-Tree that which covered; his eye swerved not, nor swept astray. Indeed, he saw one of the greatest signs of his Lord." A full description of this event and further details of the Lotus of the furthest boundary are given in Bukhari, 1:214, 4:289; and Muslim, 1:102 and 110–11. Mention of the furthest Lotus is related to the Prophet's Ascension (*mi'raj*). See Sells, "Ascension," 176–80.
3. *Qur'an* 2:285.
4. Ibid. 30:22.
5. Ibid. 3:7.
6. Bukhari, 3:151–52.
7. *Qur'an* 21:35.
8. Ibid. 3:119.
9. See ibid. 23:96.
10. See ibid. 7:159.
11. Ibid. 4:135.
12. See ibid. 2:115.

13. Ibid. 3:20.
14. Ibid. 65:11–12.
15. Ibid. 2:41.
16. Ibid. 44:3; 76:23 and 97:1.
17. Ibid. 16:102.

5. THE SENSE-OF-SELF AND THE DEBT

1. A community that accepts the Recitation accesses it through interpretations. Nobody within the community can lay claim to fullness of interpretation. As a result, consensus within the community on the good is possible only on the basis of respect for different interpretations. This is shown by a case from the time of the Prophet, narrated by 'Ali: "The Prophet sent a Sariya under the command of a human being from the Ansar and ordered soldiers to obey him. He became angry and said, 'Didn't the Prophet order you to obey me!' They replied, 'Yes.' He said, 'Collect fire-wood for me.' So they collected it. He said, 'Make a fire.' When they made it, he said, 'Enter it.' They were ready to do that too, but they began to hold each other, saying, 'We have fled to the Prophet from the fire.' They kept on saying that till the fire was extinguished and the anger of the commander abated. When the Prophet heard of it, he said, 'Had they entered it [i.e., the fire], they would not have left it till the Day of Resurrection. Obedience is required when he enjoins what is good'" (Bukhari, 5:441).
2. See *Qur'an* 45:23.
3. See ibid. 7:182.
4. See ibid. 6:80 and 20:98.
5. See ibid. 17:85.
6. See John 3:8.
7. See *Qur'an* 47:38.
8. See ibid. 17:85. That we are given only a little knowledge is a basic postulate regarding human knowledge throughout the Recitation. This is a message of the Throne Verse (2:255): "God, there is no god but He, the Living, the Upright. Slumber seizes Him not, neither sleep; to Him belongs all that is in the heavens and the earth. Who is there that shall intercede with Him save by His leave? He knows what lies before them and what is after them, and they comprehend not anything of His knowledge save such as He wills. His Throne comprises the heavens and earth; the preserving of them oppresses Him not; He is the All-high, the All-glorious."
9. When asked about the Prophet's character, his widow Aisha said, "The Recitation was his character" (Muslim, 1:359).
10. Ar. *Jibril* (Heb. *Gabri'el*) is the angel who "delivers" the proclamation of the Recitation to the heart of the prophet Muhammad (See *Qur'an* 2:97). Gabriel is mentioned three times in the Recitation (2:97–98 and 66:4). Interpreters of the Recitation, including al-Tabari, al-Zamakhshari,

and al-Baydawi, identify the messenger who delivers the revelation to the Prophet Muhammad as Gabriel. They interpret two of the Prophet's encounters mentioned in the Recitation (53:1–18) as involving Gabriel.

11. Muslim, 1:2–3.
12. See *Qur'an* 59:23.
13. See ibid. 6:163.
14. See ibid. 68:4.

6. BEING-AT-PEACE

1. God is Peace. This is stated explicitly in the Bible (Judges 6:24) and the Recitation (59:23). Although *al-Salām* is only one of the most beautiful divine names, it would appear to be decisive for understanding the entire lesson of the Debt that lies at the heart of this discussion. Connected to it are *muslim, islam,* and *aslama*. They are presented in order of progression from the human toward the Principle even though our meditations have focused on the relationship between the creative Principle and its revelation in existence. Understanding this semantic cluster would appear to be a precondition to answering major questions regarding the sources of human misery and the scope for rising above it. Arabic *salam* corresponds to the Hebrew *shālōm* and the Greek *eirēnē*. It is Peace manifesting as "wholeness," "harmony," "health," and "security," which encompass both physical and spiritual content and relate not merely to individuals but to the connections between them, entire communities, humanity, and all of existence. Here it may be seen that the relationship with Peace predetermines every condition of the individual and so of the world as a whole. This discourse attempts to preserve the semantic link by translating *al-Salām* as *Peace (Mir,* in Bosnian). It is worth noting that the terms *mil* (the Bosnian root of words meaning "dear," "gentle," and "mercy") and *mir* are connected through the Indo-European root *mei-* ("mild," "soft," "gentle") with forms in *-lo* and *-ro*. Without these forms, one gets not the Slavic, but the Sanskrit *máyas* ("cheerful"). (See Skok *Etimologijski rječnik hrvatskoga ili srpskoga jezika,* 2:428.) One cannot discuss Peace as Fullness without treating how it appears/shows itself in the totality of existence. To determine the meaning of the term "person-of-peace" *(muslim),* one must first show how and where the term "Peace" appears in the Recitation. (For the term *muslim,* see the following note.) The expression *(Qur'an* 59:23) "He is God; there is no God but He; He is the King, the All-holy, the All-peaceable, the All-faithful; the All-preserver, the All-mighty, the All-compeller, the All-sublime" entails, among other things, that there can be no peace without Peace. Humans are, accordingly, always between the absence of Peace, or the void, and Peace as Fullness. We have come into existence from that Peace and will return to It. Our turn to Peace is the discovery of our reality. The turn away from Him is covering the real or taking things

rather than the Principle for principles. To realize oneself as a human being means to return to Peace. This return corresponds to arrival in Paradise or the approach to God. The contrary is arrival in Hell or distance from God. For those who have realized themselves in Peace, return is to the Dwelling of Peace (6:127; 10:25; 56:88–91). In that Dwelling, angels call on and affirm Peace (13:23–24; 16:30–32; 39:73; 50:34), as do people to each other (10:9–10; 14:23; 19:62; 25:75; 33:41–44; 36:58; 56:25–26). Given that return to God is the breaking of all human ties with anything other than Him, the encounter is the revelation of Peace and the waning of everything associated with Him (16:87). This is the meaning of the mention of Peace before the people of Paradise (7:46; 15:45–46). The revelation of Peace to humanity takes place primarily through His prophets (37:181). Peace is with them—Noah (11:48; 37:79), Abraham (11:69; 15:51–52; 21:69; 37:109; 51:25), Elijah (37:130), Moses and Aaron (37:120), Jesus (19:15; 19:33), and Muhammad (33:56). The revelation is of Peace, with Peace, and by Peace (97:3–5), and, accordingly, it has been "sent down." The revelation ties its recipients to Peace and allows them to discover Peace as their authentic nature. Peace abides with certain of God's servants (27:59). God leads people on the paths of Peace (5:15–16), and through Him, those who accept the signs of God are linked (6:54; 11:48; 24:27; 24:61). The angels establish relations with the prophets through Peace and vice versa—the prophets with the angels (11:69; 15:51–52; 51:25). When they encounter those who do not know, the faithful invoke Peace and take refuge in Him (25:63; 28:55). The prophets are turned toward Peace, and He is their light against the coverers—Abraham (19:47), Moses and Aaron (20:46–48). Those who follow the prophets, which means those who have realized their authentic nature, establish, maintain, and change their relations with others on the basis of Peace (4:89–90; 4:94; 8:61). When such relations become impossible and all other ways have been tried, those for whom Peace is the principle of their relations with themselves, others, and the world become warriors for Peace (4:91). All that this means is the defense of Peace as our authentic nature and the purpose of all existence. Orientation toward Peace cannot be harmonized with any form of denial of Him, and those-who-are-at-Peace are expected to replace that which covers Him by Him, but never by abandoning Peace as the goal (37:34–35). That means that forgiveness and Peace are refuge from covering (43:89). Given that at the moment of death, free will is extinguished, those who have sought refuge in Peace will find confirmation of Him, while those who have covered Him, will finally witness Him (16:27–28).

2. The *muslim* (the person-of-peace) is a human being who through being-at-peace (*islam*) connects with God as Peace (*al-Salām*). Everything in existence is from God, and everything returns to Him. God is thus both Giver and Receiver. Everything we have, we have received from God and that is our debt to Him. We are, accordingly, both receivers and givers.

Consciousness of God includes recognition of the real of death, but also transcendence of it by being a person-of-peace or one who returns to God as Peace (*Qur'an* 3:102). Acceptance of humanity includes turning toward God from the position of being a person-of-peace (46:15). For the men and women of peace, God has prepared forgiveness and great reward (33:35). Being a person-of-peace entails difference from the sinner (68:35). Those who trust in God's signs and are people-of-peace gain entry to heaven (43:67–70). The coverers will finally desire that they had been people-of-peace, as all relations except with God will be extinguished (15:2). God's prophets are people-of-peace of their own free will—Noah (10:72), Abraham (3:67; 2:127–29), Ishmael (2:127–29), Joseph (12:101), Muhammad ("the First of the peaceful," 6:162–63; 27:91–92; 39:11–12). Following a prophet means being with the people-of-peace or being connected to God as Peace (3:80) through His prophets—Abraham (2:127–29; 2:133; 2:136; 3:84; 22:78; 2:132), Lot (51:35–36), Ishmael (2:127–29; 2:133; 2:136; 3:84), Jacob (2:132; 2:133; 2:136; 3:84), Moses (10:84; 2:136; 3:84; 7:125–26), Solomon (27:30–31; 27:38; 27:42–43), Jesus (2:136; 3:52–53; 3:84; 5:111), and Muhammad (11:14; 30:52–53; 29:46; 66:5; 3:64; 27:80–81; 21:108). Those who accept the Recitation and the earlier Books as having been sent down from God are people-of-peace (28:53). The Recitation is guidance, mercy, and good news for the people-of-peace and links them with the Prophet and with God (16:89; 16:102). Those who call on God and are just are people-of-peace (41:33). Consciousness of the imminence of death stimulates even the idolater to confess God's Unity and become a person-of-peace (10:90). Even the Jinns, fiery beings of free will, can be people-of-peace (72:14–15).

3. Being a person-of-peace (*muslim*) determines relations with God as Peace (*al-Salām*) through being-at-peace (*islam*). Such being confesses that there is no peace but Peace. Given that human will is conditioned or finite, while God's is absolute, our being-at-peace always entails God as Refuge. The person-of-peace relates to everything as a sign of Peace. This relating is the state denoted by the phrase being-at-peace (*islam*) or related verbal forms. Grammatically speaking, a verb is any form of the word that expresses action, being, or appearance. The modes of acting, being, or appearing as a person-of-peace in relation to God as Peace include both giving and receiving and as such can be found in several citations from the Recitation. "What, do they desire another Debt than God's, for in Him has found peace whosoever is in the heavens and the earth, willingly or unwillingly, and to Him they shall be returned?" (3:83); "Nay, but whosoever finds peace in God, being a good-doer, his wage is with his Lord, and no fear shall be on them, neither shall they sorrow" (2:112); "Turn unto your Lord and take refuge in Him, ere the chastisement come upon you, then you will not be helped" (39:54); "Say, 'God's guidance is the true guidance, and we are commanded to take refuge in the Lord of all Being'" (6:71); "Say, 'I have

been commanded to be the first of the people-of-peace, Be not thou of the idolaters'" (6:14); "Say, 'I am forbidden to serve those you call on apart from God since the clear signs came to me from my Lord; and I am commanded to seek peace in the Lord of all Being'" (40:66); "Your God is one God, and so seek peace in Him" (22:34); "Even so He perfects His blessing upon you, that haply you will be at peace" (16:81). God shows the relationship of the person-of-peace, being-at-peace, and Peace in the Recitation (2:131) through the example of the prophet Abraham, "When his Lord said to him, 'Be at peace,' he said, 'I am at peace in the Lord of all Being.'" Being-at-peace is the response of Abraham and Ishmael to God's command to Abraham to sacrifice his own son, "When they were at peace, He flung them upon his brow" (37:103). The Torah as sent down is the source and ground for judgment availed of by the prophets who have made their peace and established relations with God as Peace (5:44), cf. (3:20): "So, if they dispute with thee, say, 'I have found peace in God, and whosoever follows me.' And say to those who have been given the Book and to the common folk, 'Have you found peace?' If they have found peace, they are right guided; but if they turn their backs, thine it is only to deliver the Message; and God sees His servants." "But no, by thy Lord! They will not believe till they make thee the judge regarding the disagreement between them, then they shall find in themselves no impediment touching thy verdict, but shall be fully at peace" (4:65); "The Arabs say, 'We believe.' Say, 'You do not believe; rather say, "We are at peace"; for belief has not yet entered your hearts'" (49:14); "Say to the Arabs who were left behind, 'You shall be called against a people possessed of great might to fight them, or they will be at peace'" (48:16); "They count it as a favour to thee that they are at peace! Say, 'Do not count your being at peace as a favour to me: nay, but rather God confers a favour upon you, in that He has guided you to belief, if it be that you are truthful'" (49:17); "And halt them, to be questioned, 'Why help you not one another?' No indeed; but today they find themselves in peace and advance one upon another" (37:24–27); "She said, 'My Lord, indeed I have wronged myself, and I find peace with Solomon to God, the Lord of all Being'" (27:44); "And some of us are at peace, and some of us have deviated. Those who are at peace sought rectitude" (72:14).

4. Translator's note: Here and elsewhere the term "Sacred" translates the Bosnian word *nepovrediv*, which more literally means inviolate/inviolable. It was used by the author to translate the Arabic term *haram* in reference to *al-Masjid al-haram* or the Sacred Mosque at Mecca. The Arabic word *haram* carries connotations of purity, the forbidden, the inviolate, and the holy. As such its semantic range is similar to the Latin word *sacer*, from which is derived the modern English word "sacred."

5. "'Ali's Instructions to Malik al Ashtar," in Tabataba'i, *A Shi'ite Anthology*, 68–69. This expression of Imam 'Ali is to be found in a letter to Malik ibn al-Haris ibn al-Ashtar. It translates as follows,

Know, Malik that I am sending you to a land where governments, just and unjust, have existed before you. People will look upon your affairs in the same way that you were wont to look upon the affairs of the rulers before you. They will speak about you as you were wont to speak about those rulers. And the righteous are only known by that which God causes to pass concerning them on the tongues of His servants. So let the dearest of your treasuries be the treasury of righteous action. Control your desire and restrain your soul from what is not lawful to you, for restraint of the soul is for it to be equitous in what it likes and dislikes. Infuse your heart with mercy, love and kindness for your subjects. Be not in the face of them a voracious animal, counting them as easy prey, for they are of two kinds: either they are your brothers in debt, or your equals in creation. Error catches them unaware, deficiencies overcome them and are committed both intentionally and by mistake. So grant them your pardon and your forgiveness to the same extent that you hope God will grant you His pardon and His forgiveness. For you are above them, and he who appointed you is above you, and God is above him who appointed you. God has sought from you the fulfillment of their requirements, and He is trying you with them.

6. See *Qur'an* 47:38.
7. Ibid. 17:1.
8. Returning to Medina, after the victory at Mecca and Hunayn, the Prophet said to some of his companions, "We are returning from a small to a great war." When one of them asked, "What is the great war, Divine Messenger?"—he replied, "The war against the self!" (See Lings, *Muhammad: His Life Based on the Earliest Sources*, 330.)

7. FAITH

God commands people to flee to Him. See *Qur'an* 51:50.
2. Muslim, 1:255–56.
3. *Qur'an* 2:256.
4. See ibid. 33:72.
5. At the very root of human creaturehood is the covenant based on confidence. See ibid. 7:172 and 33:72. In the first verse, God asks us about ourselves. In the second, He offers us confidence. The possibility of a negative answer to the first and of refusal of the offer in the second case confirms the Creator's will that human beings have free choice.
6. It should be stressed that in the present writer's works the Arabic word *din* is normally translated into Bosnian as *dug*, which is roughly equivalent to the English word "debt." In English translations, the concept *din* is normally interpreted as "religion." Debt is a relationship between the debtor, on the one hand, and the creditor, on the other. The debtor has an obligation to return

what was received under conditions determined by the creditor. When what was received has been returned, an authentic relationship is established between giver and recipient. That is the original meaning of the term "religion"—"re-binding" or the establishment of an authentic relationship between parties to a contract in which one gives and the other takes. We are creatures, and both ourselves and what we do have been received from the Creator. Returning what has been received is to pay the Debt of existence or to bind with the Creator in what is first and last our highest potential.

7. *Qur'an* 13:19–21.

8. One may talk of the Absolute only if one takes into account the ontological chain—Essence, Unity, names, the imaginal, and the sensible world. Unity is Absolute. He confirms Essence. The opposite of the Absolute is void. The Creator-creature relationship does not approach void as long as multiplicity gives meaning to things in the Absolute. Witness to Unity, which may be called "adequation," is ascent through all the ontological levels toward the Absolute or the discovery of Him in everything which reveals Him. "The need for equality, which is part of the nostalgia in the soul of fallen man, is above all the need to be 'adequate' once more to the Divine Presence. This adequacy, the greatest of all Mysteries, is expressed in Islam, in the words: 'Neither My earth, nor My heaven hath room for Me, but the heart of My believing slave hath room for Me.' The highest Saints are equal in virtue of the equality of their emptinesses which receive the Fullness of the Infinite; and this equality has, underlying its Divine aspect, what might be called a celestial aspect." (Lings, *Ancient Beliefs and Modern Superstitions*, 48.)

9. See *Qur'an* 4:163–65.

10. Ibid. 5:68.

11. Muslim, 1:31.

12. Jesus told his disciples (Luke 14:26): "If any man come to me, and hate not his father, and mother, and wife, and children, and brethren, and sisters, yea, and his own life also, he cannot be my disciple."

13. See *Qur'an* 6:162–63.

14. Ibid. 3:31.

15. See ibid. 3:109 and 5:17–18.

16. See ibid. 112:1.

17. See ibid. 33:21.

18. See ibid. 68:4.

19. See ibid. 33:46.

20. See ibid. 6:163.

8. BEAUTY

1. Muslim, 1:53.

2. Bukhari, 8:336–37.

3. It is worth stressing that the meditations presented in this book are based on restoration of the semantic connections between the concepts *al-Salām*, *muslim*, *islam*, and *aslama*. The translations offered here: peace,

person-of-peace, being-at-peace, and to be-at-peace have been chosen as a possible interpretation that preserves the semantic chain derived from the verbal root *slm*. Other translations of these terms are possible and are to be met with in current translations and dictionaries. The option offered here does not exhaust the various possibilities, but it serves to establish and stress the importance of preserving semantic links over different textual contexts. On the various possibilities for interpretation of these terms, which appear in the Recitation some 120 times, see the following: Bravmann, *The Spiritual Background of Early Islam: Studies in Ancient Arab Concepts*; Künstlinger, "Islām, Muslim, aslama im Kurān"; Robson, "Islam as a Term"; Izutsu, *Ethico-Religious Concepts in the Qur'an*; Smith, *An Historical and Semantic Study of the Term "Islam" as Seen in a Sequence of Qur'an Commentaries*.

4. For more on the relationship between witness to Unity and associating with God/idolatry see Chapter 2, note 1. As pointed out, idolatry may take various forms. The most important, however, is covered or invisible association unto God. One day, the Prophet went out from his house and found his companions discussing the Antichrist (false Messiah). He said, "Shall I tell you of something that frightens me more than the Antichrist?", and the men replied that he should. He said, "Covered idolatry!—in other words, that someone pray and appear to do so well because someone is watching" (Ibn Mājja, 2:146, tradition no. 4204).

5. *Qur'an* 68:4.

6. See Muslim, 1:359.

7. Bukhari, 8:35.

8. Ibid. 5:71.

9. Ibid. 3:492.

10. Malik, 438.

11. The following names of God correspond to the examples cited: *al-Tawwab, al-Mu'min, al-Ghaffar, al-Halim, al-Wadud, al-Sabur, al-Hakim.*

9. THE HOUR

1. Muslim, 4:1526.

2. Ibid. 4:1363. See Chittick, *The Sufi Path of Knowledge*, 292, n. 33; and Graham, *The Divine Word and Prophetic Word in Early Islam*, 178–80.

3. See *Qur'an* 28:70; 30:18; 64:1.

4. Ibid. 17:44.

5. See ibid. 11:73.

6. Ibid. 3:83.

7. Ibid. 2:186.

8. Ibid. 50:16.

9. Muslim, 4:1217.

10. *Qur'an* 16:77. See also 54:50.

11. Ibid. 2:123. See also 82:19.
12. Ibid. 99:6–8.
13. See ibid. 3:9 and 4:140.
14. See ibid. 40:52.
15. Hujwiri, *Kashf al-mahjub*, 231.

10. HUMANITY

1. See *Qur'an* 49:13; 6:98.
2. See ibid. 5:48.
3. See ibid. 2:115 and 2:186.
4. See ibid. 57:4.
5. See ibid. 40:7.
6. See ibid. 50:16.
7. See ibid. 2:186.
8. See ibid. 23:44.
9. See ibid. 2:115.
10. Ibid. 34:9.
11. Ibid. 5:32.
12. Ibid. 31:28.
13. Ibid. 2:213. See also 21:92.
14. Ibid. 10:47.
15. Ibid. 6:132.
16. Bukhari, 8:35.

11. THE OTHER AND THE DIFFERENT

1. *Qur'an* 29:46. (See also 16:125.) This article is of crucial importance for our meditation. First, it is a command to those who accept the Prophet the Praised and the Recitation sent down to him. Second, the command informs discussion with others in the best way. Third, it defines those others as those to whom their own Books have been sent down. Fourth, these followers of the Book are measured purely on the basis of their doing or not doing evil. Fifth, the command confirms that different ways to God exist. Sixth, the variety of ways confirms that God is one and the same. Seventh, accepting these implications of God's command is both cause and consequence of being a person-of-peace—of being one who connects with God as Peace through being-at-peace.
2. *Qur'an* 3:113–15.
3. Ibid. 10:19.
4. Ibid. 10:47.
5. Ibid. 14:4.
6. Ibid. 21:25.
7. Ibid. 22:34.

8. Ibid. 5:48.

9. Jews and Christians are the major others of the entire divine discourse as given in the Recitation. They are two of the peoples of the Books sent down by God. Given that, according to the word of God, the Recitation was sent down in similar ways before, the communities of the Jews and Christians, already formed by it and through their historical experience, are taken as patterns for the destiny of a people of the Book. This experience appears to the community of the people of the Recitation in the form of its own potential to adhere to the demands of the Book, rather than any others, or to reject it, and a number of other possibilities. Every Book received exists in particular relation to the individual and the people. This is how it can be accepted and applied even in ways quite contrary to the Book's inner contents. If Jews direct their relations by the Torah, Christians by the Gospel, everything the Recitation has to say about their experiences relates equally to the potential and experience of Muslims who direct their relations by the Recitation. There is no rebuke against the Jews or Christians that cannot be understood at the same time and beforehand as a rebuke of the muslim.

10. *Qur'an* 22:40.

11. Ibid. 3:64.

12. Ibid. 41:34.

13. Ibid. 4:69.

14. See Bayhaqi, 9:4.

15. See Muslim, 4:1260.

16. See *Qur'an* 10:47 and 16:36.

17. See ibid. 14:4.

18. See ibid. 37:171.

19. See ibid. 3:79.

20. See ibid. 2:37 and 110:3.

21. See ibid. 4:64 and 9:104.

22. See ibid. 66:8 and 2:222.

23. See *Qur'an* 7:23. Adam was created in beautiful uprightness, which corresponds to the condition of Paradise. God allowed him to eat of whatever he wanted in the Garden, except of one tree. Adam's will was thus also God's. His entire being, with everything he did or did not do, was from God. But when Adam opposed his will to God's by laying claim to the forbidden tree, he lost his original uprightness and fell to the lowest depth. At that depth, in very contact with void, he received doctrine and ritual as the means to return to his lost and beautiful uprightness. The depth to which he fell is also the beginning of his return or ascent. This depth or beginning is symbolized by the Sacred Mosque in the Valley of Bekka and the associated rituals. Return to God is through Paradise to His Face, which never fades. The symbol of that return is the Furthest Mosque on the Mount. Both mosques were raised by Adam as signs of our fall and return. It was the Praised who fully realized the interpretation of them.

24. See *Qur'an* 11:45.
25. See ibid. 9:114 and 11:75.
26. See ibid. 4:125.
27. This name corresponds to the Arabic *al-Sabūr*. It is included in the list of ninety-nine divine names, even though it is not to be found in the Recitation. See Gardet, *'al-asmā' al-husnā,'* 1:717.
28. See *Qur'an* 7:128.
29. Ibid. 2:138.
30. See ibid. 11:73.

12. INTOLERANCE I

1. On the relationship between the clear and the unclear, that which can be proved and that which cannot in issues of faith, in the writings of John Hick and Seyyed Hossein Nasr, see Aslan, *Religious Pluralism in Christian and Islamic Philosophy*, especially the chapter "Knowledge and the Ultimate."
2. See *Qur'an* 2:31.
3. See ibid. 25:7.
4. Ibid. 16:51.
5. Ibid. 5:51. This verse is often taken out of the context of the Recitation and used for purposes which are contrary to morality. According to the Recitation, Jews and Christians dispose of everything required for redemption. Their historical experience also shows how, even with such a heritage, the centrality of God and memory of it may be lost in their communities. In the Recitation (8:27–28), God points to the similar danger of love for one's own children that excludes God, "O believers, betray not God and the Messenger, and betray not your trusts and that wittingly; and know that your wealth and your children are a trial, and that with God is a mighty wage." The command not to take Jews and Christians as friends (Arabic *awliya'*, which may also be translated as "allies") covers the maintenance of relations with God as a condition of moral connection with all people. This condition does not cover community, children, or property, as, whenever they are taken to the exclusion of God, they are a temptation and enemy of the faithful. No worldly tie is acceptable, regardless of whom it is with, if the person-of-peace resiles from moral honesty. This is stressed explicitly (3:10), "As for the coverers, their riches will not avail them, neither their children, aught against God; those—they shall be fuel for the Fire." And even more explicitly (9:24), "Say, 'If your fathers, your sons, your brothers, your wives, your clan, your possessions that you have gained, commerce you fear may slacken, dwellings you love—if these are dearer to you than God and His Messenger, and to struggle in his way, then wait till God brings His command; God guides not the people of the ungodly.'" Jesus makes

clear reference to this same attitude toward the other, whether close or distant, insofar as it excludes Unity as the principle which informs human character (Luke 14:26).

6. *Qur'an* 2:111.

7. Ibid. 62:5. This verse, like the others in this chapter, offers a general pattern for the relationship between the Book and the people who have inherited it. Given that all people—including Jews, Christians, and Muslims—have equal dignity in principle, their potential to discover or cover this dignity is also equal. The reference to the relationship to the Torah in the verse is a general one, and the message is equally valid for the Gospel or the *Qur'an*. Comments regarding Jews and Christians are equally applicable to Muslims and other peoples of the Book.

8. *Qur'an* 5:68.

9. Ibid. 2:75.

10. Ibid. 4:46. See, also, 2:59; 5:13; 5:41; 7:162.

11. Ibid. 5:82.

12. Ibid. 3:67–68.

13. God mentions these four communities in the Recitation (22:17). While they are not the only examples determined by common principles over against the differences between them, one should make clear who the Sabaeans and Magians are. The Sabaeans appear to have been a monotheist religious group intermediate between Judaism and Christianity. Their name (probably derived from the Aramaic verb *tsĕbha'*, to be immersed) signifies that they were the followers of John the Baptist. In this case, they could be identified with the Mandaeans, a community which can still be found to this day in Iraq. They should not be identified with the so-called Sabaeans of Harran, a Gnostic sect which still existed during the first centuries A.H. and which consciously assumed the name of the true Sabaeans to ensure advantages which Muslims gave the followers of monotheist religions (Asad, *The Message of the Qur'an*, 14, n.49). The Magians (*al-majus*) were followers of Zarathustra or Zoroaster (Zardusht), the Iranian prophet who lived around the middle of the last millennium before Christ and whose teachings are inscribed in the *Zend-Avesta*. Today, they are represented by the Gabri in Iran and, even more, by the Parsees in India and Pakistan. Their religion, although dualist in its philosophy, is based on faith in God as the Creator of the Worlds (ibid., 507, n. 19).

14. *Qur'an* 9:97.

15. Ibid. 9:99.

16. See ibid. 5:44.

17. See ibid. 4:79.

18. See ibid. 21:107.

19. Ibid. 3:18–19.

20. Ibid. 9:33.

13. INTOLERANCE II

1. *Qur'an* 7:168–70.
2. Ibid. 9:71.
3. See ibid. 45:23.
4. Imam 'Ali ibn Abu Talib, describing the true people-of-peace, said, "They are dissatisfied with the insignificance of their good deeds and they consider the number of their deeds insufficient. They always reprove themselves and are cautious with their actions. When one of them is praised, he fears that which is said of him and says, 'I know myself better than others, and my Lord knows me better than I know myself. O, God, do not deal with me according to what they say and make me better than what they think of me and forgive me what they do not know'" (*Nahjul Balagha*, 334).
5. *Qur'an* 3:175.
6. See ibid. 16:125.
7. See ibid. 25:63 and 28:55.
8. See ibid. 6:108.
9. See ibid. 2:190–93.
10. Ibid. 5:13.
11. Ibid. 3:146.
12. Ibid. 41:14.
13. Ibid. 109:1–6.
14. Ibid. 9:23.

14. THE MUSLIM

1. For more on the intellectual, ideological, political, geo-strategic, and cultural aspects of the Muslim question, see: Mahmutćehajić, *Learning from Bosnia: Approaching Tradition*; idem, "With the Other"; idem, "Sameness in Diversity: The Religio Perennis in Judaism, Christianity and Islam"; idem, "Islam, Catholicism and Orthodoxy: The Matrices of Conceptual Transfer"; and Waardenburg, *Muslims and Others: Relations in Context*.
2. In his investigations of the inappropriateness of contemporary ideas, e.g., religion, for the study and representation of difference in the world, Wilfred Cantwell Smith has made great efforts at reexamination. See Smith, *The Meaning and the End of Religion*.
3. These two points of view, the traditional and the modern, relate differently to the issue of sincerity. Although the traditional point of view may consider the individual to be related to God, he may never present his word as final and independent of the interpretations of the community. The approach to revelation is always through a conditioned or finite sense-of-self and so is through the individual. All of Adam's children are needed for this. From the modern point-of-view, the individual may claim the right to take his own world picture as correct and final. This individual does not consider

himself an (other's) agent or mediator in authentic creation which is repeated from moment to moment. His picture is final so that a finite work is always presented as proof of sincerity.

4. The prevailing representations of the muslim and *islam* arose out of the tensions and conflicts between the "Muslim" peoples and the "Christian West." The histories of both sides discuss them as though they were fully known things. If, however, that knowledge is considered from another point-of-view—say Taoism or Confucianism—one may arrive at a different picture of that which only seems known. See, for example, Murata, *The Tao of Islam: A Sourcebook on Gender Relationship in Islamic Thought*; idem, *Chinese Gleams of Sufi Light*; Izutsu, *Sufism and Taoism: A Comparative Study of Key Philosophical Concepts*.

5. *Qur'an* 41:33.

6. Ibid. 2:132.

7. Ibid. 10:84.

8. Ibid. 12:101.

9. Ibid. 5:111.

10. Ibid. 16:102.

11. Ibid. 6:162–63.

12. Ibid. 59:22–24.

13. Ibid. 25:63.

14. Ibid. 5:15–16.

15. Ibid. 10:9–10.

16. Ibid. 28:52–55. Interpreting verse 6:54, in which the formula *al-Salām 'alaikum* ("peace be with you") appears, Fakhr al-Din al-Razi stresses that in all cases of this expression in the Recitation, *al-Salām* should be read as a divine name. (See Razi, *Mafatih al-ghaib*, 3:54). God orders that the Prophet accept and relate to others the obligation to greet in peace (see *Qur'an* 24:27, 24:61 and others) which is analogous to Jesus' order to his disciples (Luke 10:5–6), "And into whatsoever house ye enter, first say, Peace be to this house. And if the son of peace be there, your peace shall rest upon it: if not, it shall turn to you again."

17. *Qur'an* 43:89.

18. Ibid. 4:94.

19. Tabarsi, *Mishkat ul-Anwar Fi Ghurar il-Akhbar*, 310–11.

20. See *Qur'an* 59:23.

21. The Prophet says, "This world is damned. Damned too is all that is in it—except remembrance of God and that which is related with it, and the learned, and the learning" (Tirmidhi, *al-Jami' al-sahih wa huwa sunan al-Tirmidhi*, 4:561, tradition 2322). Consciousness of human debt returns human being from remoteness to nearness, from difference to sameness, from multiplicity to unity, from anger to mercy, from darkness to light, from disorder to Peace. The whole of creation reveals unity in multiplicity. Everything that is in multiplicity is a sign of unity. If one sees in it anything

other than discourse of unity, then these things in creation have been taken outside of their authentic and only true sense. Then, as the Prophet says, they are damned both individually and collectively. Their only meaning is to remind or speak of their Creator. Reminiscence is everything that turns people to God and everything that ensures they are in their right mind with regard to Him. If the world, or anything in it, is not such a reminder, then it is association with God, the greatest sin, and therefore the greatest curse.

22. Humanity's relationship with God is decisive for understanding all the language of the Recitation. According to the scheme "person-of-peace (*muslim*)—being-at-peace (*islam*) —Peace (*al-Salām*)," every human condition may be brought into relationship with God's names. We realize ourselves through discovery of our finest nature or realization of the most beautiful divine names. This relationship between human being and God realizes our covenant. The name "Christian" is to be understood in terms of this relationship. Those who realize their being anointed (christened) through the Anointed (the Christ, Messiah), as the finest example in relationship with God the Anointer, enjoy "anointing" (christening) as that link or relationship. In the Recitation (2:137–38), God talks of this: "And if they believe in the like of that you believe in, then they are truly guided; but if they turn away, then they are clearly in schism; God will suffice you for them; He is the All-hearing, the All-knowing; the anointment of God; and who is there that anoints fairer than God? Him we are serving."

23. *Qur'an* 5:3.
24. Ibid. 3:19.
25. Ibid. 3:85.
26. Ibid. 6:125.
27. Ibid. 39:22.
28. Ibid. 61:7.
29. Ibid. 49:17.
30. On the relationship between human nature and the most beautiful names of God, see Chittick, *The Sufi Path of Knowledge*, 21–22.
31. See *Qur'an* 41:34.

15. THE UNIVERSALITY OF PROPHECY

1. Murata and Chittick, *The Vision of Islam: The Foundations of Muslim Faith and Practice*, 164.
2. *Qur'an* 6:112–13.
3. See ibid. 38:75.
4. Ibid. 21:25.
5. Ibid. 10:47.
6. Ibid. 14:4.
7. Ibid. 5:48.
8. Ibid. 2:136. See also 2:285 and 3:84.

16. THE NATION OF THE JUST

1. *Qur'an* 15:10–11.
2. Bukhari, 9:482.
3. See *Qur'an* 7:156.
4. See ibid. 2:70; 6:80; 20:98.
5. Ibid. 17:85.
6. See Mark 3:28–30; Matthew 12:31–32; Luke 12:10.
7. See *Qur'an* 4:48 and 116.
8. Ibid. 35:15.
9. See ibid. 56:7–10.
10. Ibid. 5:66.
11. Ibid. 3:113–15.
12. Ibid. 3:75.
13. To determine this, we adopt the Talmudic concept *Hasidei Ummot ha-Olam* ("the Just of the nations of the world") (*Babylonian Talmud*, Sanhedrin 105a). See Telushkin, *Jewish Literacy*, 410–13.
14. Bukhari, 3:108. See Wensinck, *Concordance et indices de la tradition musulmane*, 1:486.
15. *Qur'an* 2:177.

17. DIALOGUE

1. *Qur'an* 28:77.
2. Ibid. 2:195.
3. Ibid. 17:7.
4. Ibid. 4:125.
5. Ibid. 29:46.
6. Ibid. 2:109.
7. Ibid. 25:63. See also 28:55.
8. Ibid. 3:64.
9. Ibid. 6:108.
10. *Nahjul Balagha*, 89.
11. Ar. *Umm al-Kitāb*.
12. Nasr, *The Need for a Sacred Science*, 56–57.
13. *Qur'an* 89:27–30.

18. FINDING FAULT WITH OTHERS AND THE SELF

1. *Qur'an* 2:216.
2. See ibid. 67:3–4.
3. Ibid. 35:3.
4. Ibid. 23:14.
5. Ibid. 37:96.

6. The note on the difference between sacred and profane art also delineates the contradiction between tradition, as understood in this discussion, and modernity, which takes human being as the heart of all existence. Absolute Peace is always present in everything. So it is with human being taken as a thing, but it is otherwise with regards to our free will. Our goal is Absolute Peace, toward which we may be directed at any moment but with which we may never be equated. Here it is possible to see why remembrance and connection are of decisive importance in traditional learning and ritual based on it. As individuals, we may never be sure of our own sincerity. Whatever we know is repeated countless times, transcending us in space and time. "The world is damned," says the Prophet, "along with everything in it, except remembrance." But, we are in the world and so constantly liable to forgetting. Our sincerity is always in question. The modern, ideological image of our relationship to the world is entirely different. We are sure of our sincerity, as we refuse the piecemeal nature of our knowledge. And so we can explain why it is that the fundamentalist point-of-view does not tolerate any form of remembrance or holy art.

7. *Qur'an* 7:16.
8. Ibid. 7:23.
9. Ibid. 2:37.
10. Ibid. 45:23.
11. Ibid. 67:3–4.
12. Ibid. 40:64.
13. Ibid. 95:4–6.
14. See Muslim, 1:53.
15. See *Qur'an* 37:96.
16. For our inability to regard the world and ourselves at the same time and the distortion of the world because of our own undisclosure, see Rumi, *The Mathnawi*, 2:81–83.
17. See *Qur'an* 19:93.
18. Ibid. 3:79.

19. FREE WILL AND THE COVENANT

1. *Qur'an* 20:115.
2. Ibid. 2:35–36.
3. See ibid. 7:22; 20:121.
4. Ibid. 5:97.
5. Ibid. 2:144.
6. Ibid. 17:1.
7. Ibid. 7:172–73.
8. See ibid. 2:84; 3:187; 5:14; 13:20; 57:8.
9. Ibid. 11:110.
10. Ibid. 11:118.

AFTERWORD: THE TEXT AND ITS POWER

1. *Qur'an* 14:4.
2. For more on muslim views of Revelation (*wahy*), see Rahman, *Prophecy in Islam.* The issue of the levels of humanity up to prophethood has been addressed by, amongst others, Ibn Khaldun. See idem, *The Muqaddimah: An Introduction to History*, 75–78.
3. Fadl, *The Place of Tolerance in Islam*, 107–8.
4. *Qur'an* 5:8. Comparable passages exist in the Torah and the Gospels for this fundamental ethical position in the Recitation. For more see Mahmutćehajić, "Sameness in Diversity." Two examples may be given here of this ethical principle, one from the Torah and another from the Gospels. "Ye shall do no unrighteousness in judgment: Thou shalt not respect the person of the poor, nor honour the person of the mighty: but in righteousness shalt thou judge thy neighbour" (Leviticus 19:15); and "Woe unto you, scribes and Pharisees, hypocrites! For ye pay tithe of mint and anise and cummin, and have omitted the weightier matters of the law, judgment, mercy, and faith: these ought ye to have done, and not to leave the other undone" (Matthew 23:23).

Bibliography

Ahsan, Maimul. *Human Rights in the Muslim World: Fundamentalism, Constitutionalism, and International Politics.* Khan Durham: Carolina Academic Press, 2003.

'Ali Ibn Abu Talib, Imam. "Instructions to Mālik al-Ashtar." In Tabatabā'i, *A Shi'ite Anthology*, 68–82. Translated by William C. Chittick. Qum: Ansariyan Publications, 1989.

————. *Nahjul Balagha: Sermons, Letters and Sayings*, translated by Syed Ali Raza. Qum: Ansariyan Publications, 1989.

Arberry, Arthur J. *The Koran Interpreted.* London: George Allen & Unwin, 1980.

Asad, Muhammad. *The Message of the Qur'an,* Gibraltar: Dar al-Andalus, 1980.

Aslan, Adnan. *Religious Pluralism in Christian and Islamic Philosophy.* London: Routledge Curzon, 2004.

Bayhaqī, Abu Bakr al-Khusrawdjirdī, al-. *Al-Sunan al-Kubrā.* 10 vols. Beirut: Dar al-Kutub al-'Ilmiyya, 1994.

Bravmann, Meir M. *The Spiritual Background of Early Islam: Studies in Ancient Arab Concepts.* Leiden: E. J. Brill, 1972.

Bukhari, Imam al-. *Sahih al-Bukhari*, translated by Muhammad Muhsin Khan. 9 vols. Beirut: Dal al-Arabia, 1985.

Chittick, William C. *The Sufi Path of Knowledge: Ibn al-'Arabi's Metaphysics of Imagination.* Albany: SUNY Press, 1989.

The Encyclopaedia of the Qur'an. 1 vol. Leiden: Brill, 2001.

The Encyclopedia of Islam. New ed. 1 vol. Leiden: E. J. Brill, 1986.

Fadl, Khaled Abou el-. *The Place of Tolerance in Islam.* Boston: Beacon Press, 2002.

Friedmann, Yohanan. *Tolerance and Coercion in Islam: Interfaith Relations in the Muslim Tradition.* Cambridge: Cambridge University Press, 2003.

Gardet, Louis. "'al-asma al-husna." In *The Encyclopedia of Islam*, new ed., 1 vol. Leiden: E. J. Brill, 1986, 714–17.

Gopin, Marc. *Between Eden and Armageddon: The Future of World Religions, Violence and Peacemaking.* Oxford: Oxford University Press, 2000.

Graham, William A. *The Divine Word and Prophetic Word in Early Islam.* The Hague: Mouton, 1977.

Heyd, David, ed. *Toleration: An Elusive Virtue.* Princeton: Princeton University Press, 1996.

Hujwiri, 'Ali al-. *Kashf al-mahjub*, edited by V. Zhukovsky. Tehran: Amir Kabir, 1957.

Ibn Hanbal, Ahmad. *al-Musnad.* Beirut: Dar Sādîr.

Ibn Khaldūn, Wali al-Din 'Abd al-Rahman. *The Muqaddimah: An Introduction to History*, translated by Franz Rosenthal. London: Routledge and Kegan Paul, 1958.

Ibn Mājja. *Sunan*, edited by Muhammad Fu'ād 'Abd al-Bāqī. 2 vols. Beirut: Dar al-Fikr.

Izutsu, Toshihiko. *Ethico-Religious Concepts in the Qur'an.* Montreal: McGill University Press, 1996.

———. *God and Man in the Qur'an: Semantics of the Qur'anic Weltanschauung.* Tokyo: Keio Institute of Culutral and Linguistic Studies, 1964.

———. *Sufism and Taoism: A Comparative Study of Key Philosophical Concepts.* Berkeley: University of California Press, 1984.

Kamen, Henry. *The Rise of Toleration.* New York: McGraw Hill, 1967.

Katz, Jacob. *Exclusiveness and Tolerance.* New York: Schocken Books, 1961.

Khan, Maimul. *Human Rights in the Muslim World: Fundamentalism, Constitutionalism, and International Politics.* Durham: Carolina Academic Press, 2003.

Künstlinger, Dawid. "'Islām, Muslim, aslama im Kurān." *Rocznik Orjentalistyczny* 11 (1935): 128–37.

Larsen, John Cristian. *Religious Toleration: The Variety of Rites from Cyrus to DeFoe.* New York: St. Martin's Press, 1999.

Lings, Martin. *Ancient Beliefs and Modern Superstitions*, London: Unwin Paperbacks, 1980.

———. *Muhammad: His Life Based on the Earliest Sources.* London: Unwin Human Limited, 1988.

Mahmutćehajić, Rusmir. "Fundamentalism versus Traditional Intellectuality." *Sophia: The Journal of Traditional Studies* 12/1 (2006): 33–54.

———. "Islam, Catholicism and Orthodoxy: The Matrices of Conceptual Transfer." *Sacred Web: A Journal of Tradition and Modernity* 14 (2004):17–69.

————. *Learning from Bosnia: Approaching Tradition.* New York: Fordham University Press, 2005.

————. "Sameness in Diversity: The Religio Perennis in Judaism, Christianity and Islam." *Sophia: The Journal of Traditional Studies* 10/2 (2004): 43–103.

————. "With the Other." *Sophia: The Journal of Traditional Studies* 9/2 (2003/2004): 25–76.

Makkī, Abū Tālib al-. *Qut al-qulūb.* Cairo: Mustafā al-Bābī al-Halabī, 1961.

Malik, Imam. *Al-Muwatta,* translated by 'A'isha 'Abdarahman at-Tarjumana and Ya'qub Jonson. London: Diwan Press, 1982.

Mendus, Susan. *Toleration and the Limits of Liberalism.* London: Macmillan, 1989.

Mendus, Susan, ed. *Justifying Toleration: Conceptual and Historical Perspectives.* Cambridge: Cambridge University Press, 1988.

Murata, Sachiko. *Chinese Gleams of Sufi Light.* Albany: SUNY Press, 2000.

————. *The Tao of Islam: A Sourcebook on Gender Relationship in Islamic Thought.* Albany: SUNY Press, 1992.

Murata, Sachiko and William C. Chittick. *The Vision of Islam: The Foundations of Muslim Faith and Practice.* London: J. B. Taurus, 1995.

Muslim, Imam. *Sahih Muslim,* translated by 'Abdul Hamid Siddiqi. 4 vols. Riyadh: International Islamic Publishing House.

Nasr, Seyyed Hossein. *The Need for a Sacred Science.* London: Curzon Press, 1993.

Qāshāni, 'Abd al-Razzāq al-. *A Glossary of Sufi Technical Terms,* translated by Nabil Safwat. London: Octagon Press, 1991.

Rahman, Fazlur. *Prophecy in Islam.* London: George Allen & Unwin, 1957.

Razi, Fakhr al-Din al-. *Mafatiu al-ghayb* or *Kitab al-Tafsir al-kabir.* 6 vols. Cairo: Al-Matba' al-miøriyya al-amiriyya, 1278.

Remer, Gary. *Humanism and the Rhetoric of Toleration.* University Park, Penn: Pennsylvania State University Press, 1996.

Robson, James. "Islam as a Term." *The Muslim World* 44 (1954): 101–9.

Rumi, Jalalu'ddin. *The Mathnawi,* translated by Reynold A. Nicholson. 2 vols. London: Luzac, 1977.

Sachedina, Abdulaziz. *Islamic Roots of Democratic Pluralism.* Oxford: Oxford University Press, 2001.

Sadri, Mahmoud, and Ahmad Sadri, eds. *Reason, Freedom, and Democracy in Islam: Essential Writings of 'Abdolkarim Soroush.* New York: Oxford University Press, 2000.

Said, Abdul Aziz and Meena Sharify-Funk, eds. *Cultural Diversity and Islam.* Lanham, Md: University Press of America, 2003.

Schuon, Frithjof. *Spiritual Perspectives and Human Facts.* Pates Manor: Perennial Books Limited, 1987.

Seligman, Adam B. *Modest Claim: Dialogues and Essays on Tolerance and Tradition.* Notre Dame, Ind.: University of Notre Dame Press, 2004.

Sells, Michael. "Ascension." In *Encyclopedia of the Qur'an*. 1 vol. Leiden: E. J. Brill, 2001, 176–80.

Skok, Petar. *Etimologijski rječnik hrvatskoga ili srpskoga jezika*. Zagreb: Akademija Znanosti i Umjetnosti, 1971–74.

Smith, Jane J. *An Historical and Semantic Study of the Term "Islam" as Seen in a Sequence of Qur'an Commentaries*. Missoula, Mont.: Scholars Press, 1975.

Smith, Wilfred Cantwell. *The Meaning and the End of Religion*. Minneapolis: Fortress Press, 1991.

Tabarsi, Hassan ibn Fazl ibn Hassan. *Mishkat ul-Anwar fi Ghurar il-Akhbar (The Lamp Niche for the Best Traditions)*, translated by Lisa Zaynab Morgan and Ali Peiravi. Qum: Ansariyan Publications, 2002.

Tabataba'i, Sayyid Muhammad Husayn, ed. 'Ali's Instructions to Mālik al-Ashtar. *A Shi'ite Anthology*, translated by William C. Chittick. Qum: Ansariyan Publications, 1989.

Telushkin, Rabbi Joseph. *Jewish Literacy*. New York: Harper Collins, 2001.

The Thompson Chain-Reference Bible: King James Version. Indianapolis: B. B. Kirkbride Bible Company, 1988.

Tirmidhi, Muhammad b. 'Isa Abū 'Isa al-. *al-Jami' al-sahih wa huwa sunan al-Tirmidhi*, edited by Ahmad M. Shakir. Cairo: al-Maktabat al-Islamiyya, 1938.

Waardenburg, Jacques. *Muslims and Others: Relations in Context*. Berlin: Walter de Gruyter, 2003.

Walzer, Michael. *On Toleration*. New Haven: Yale University Press, 1997.

Wensinck, Arnt J., J. P. Mensing, and J. Brugman. *Concordance et indices de la tradition musulmane*. Leiden: E. J. Brill, 1936–1969.

Conceptual Glossary

This essay on the other and otherness from a muslim point-of-view rests on three assumptions:

Anything said in one language can be translated into any other.

Translation from one language into another is never final because language is a trajectory plotted on two axes: one representing the age to which its living users belong, and the other representing transmission and change over the long chain of generations. Dependence on received concepts and the associated semantic fields all too often hinders the flow of meaning that language should serve.

So it is with language. It subsists within the horizon of the society or people that uses it, in a history of unbroken transmission from one generation to another. The mysterious revelation of God to human beings takes place in language. God reveals His discourse to a chosen individual, who, as God's prophet, passes it on in his own language, the living language of his people, to those around him and through them to others, of both that time and future generations through history. Divine discourse is thus present in human language, both as Text (the *Torah*, the *Gospels*, and the *Qur'an*, for example) and as infinite interpretation. Through links between two fundamentally different ontological levels, the human and the divine, a transformation of the semantic takes place in every language.

These three assumptions about language and translation inform this book and the author's attempt to unfold the deeper meanings of received concepts and provide them with something approaching a new translation. Readers accustomed to the treatment normally given to these concepts may find this confusing at first and may even think that the attempt obscures existing knowledge, in spite of the author's intention to clarify aspects of otherness. Such an appearance is understandable. This book treats phenomena, discourses, and texts drawn from across a millennium of history and an indeterminate metahistorical period. Contemporary human beings are unaccustomed to the perennial. Our conceptions are secular and time-bound, as contemporary humanity is all too prone to assume that the language we use differs radically from that of our ancestors a few generations ago, never mind the language used more than a thousand years ago.

As all the concepts in this book are related back to semantic kernels that clarify the connections between these concepts and how they are used in different expressions, a presentation and brief explanation of these concepts may be helpful for readers, who might otherwise be confused by our attempt to retranslate something that seems to them already known. This glossary may serve to remind the reader of an old rule of translation, involving the following steps: isolate the concepts to consider them in their different semantic contexts; determine concepts with similar or the same meanings and identify the minor semantic differences between them; determine and isolate concepts with completely opposite meanings and then find the concepts closest to them; and finally, determine the semantic fields of each of these concepts and their relations with other concepts. In this way, it should be possible to free the perennial content of language from the reductionism of contemporary secularism. Such a distinction is the condition for grasping what this discourse has to say.

Only in this way can we preserve the semantic relation between the connotations of words in the source language and those they receive during translation into another language. In this way, connections may be established among different cultures, ages, and ideas as they are transmitted as intricate complexities along the axis of the world and through the ages. In this way, we can understand and learn from the meaning of ancient discourse even today. This is because humanity is always one and the same, whatever changes it has been subjected to through the ages.

This glossary of terms presents the reader with some hints regarding the concepts behind the terms, which are drawn from contemporary language. This list also indicates the corresponding words from the language of the *Qur'an* to show that contemporary language is dependent on a current that flows through the centuries and millennia. Finally, these terms provide a context for the story of one human being, who, like every other, has received language into himself, endowing it with his substance, so that it takes on the color of his never-to-be-repeated particularity.

'abd ar. v. Servant or bondsman.

Abraham (ar. *Ibrāhīm*): A prophet of God, father of the prophets Ishmael and Isaac, restorer of the Ka'ba and the Hajj.

Absolute: Used in the traditional sense of idealist philosophy to designate unconditioned or infinite Being, which is to say Reality or God. The Absolute is fullness of Being, and so it is in opposition to the void, nothingness, or deficiency as the nonexistent other pole of Existence. Existence is conditioned, determinate, or finite being and so comprises the various "worlds" or levels of Existence, which are spread out between the Absolute and the void. Human being is finite being, which tends toward or aspires to fullness of Being or the Absolute.

Adam (ar. *Ādam*): The first human being and first prophet of God.

Aisha: Daughter of Abu Bakr, wife of the prophet Muhammad, mother of the faithful and the subject of many traditions.

Ākhira ar. v. Other World.

Ali, son of Abu Talib: Companion and son-in-law of the Prophet Muhammad, Imam, and Caliph.

All-merciful (ar. *al-Raḥmān*): Divine name and term for God as well as for an individual whose character is brought to realization in relation to mercy or Merciful God.

Almighty (ar. *al-Qādir*): Divine name of God Almighty.

Angel (ar. *malak*): (Heavenly) messenger.

Anointed (ar. *masīḥ*): The perfect human being, whose nature is realized or disclosed in relationship with God the Anointer. Anointment signifies the right relationship with, selection by, and approval by God.

'aql ar. v. Intellect and reason.

Arrogance (ar. *kibr*): The condition of elation or sufficiency in human nature, whereby dependence on God is ignored or misrecognized and consequently relationship with God as the Highest or Ultimate Principle is destroyed.

Attribute (ar. *ṣifat*): Description, quality, characteristic; a descriptive term properly applied to God, usually as a name (ar. *ism*). Attributes or names are the complementary of Essence, which is God Himself, without names or description.

āyat ar. v. Sign.

Beautiful or Good (ar. *al-Muḥsin*): Divine name and term for God as well as for an individual whose character is brought to realization through beauty and goodness or relationship with God the Beautiful and Good.

Beauty or Goodness (ar. *iḥsān*): The relationship of human being as beautiful (good) to God the Beautiful (Good).

Being (ar. *wujūd*): Being strictly belongs to God alone; more loosely, it is that which signifies God and so everything aside from Him; the illusion that anything has being independent of God is radical misrecognition of the human condition and the ultimate source of suffering; the remedy for such suffering is to turn from false being and persist in authentic being.

Being-at-Peace (ar. *islām*): The relationship of the person-of-peace with God as Peace.

Body (ar. *jism*): The lowest of the three levels—body, soul, and spirit; corresponds to earth in the external world.

Book (ar. *kitāb*): The revelation of God to humankind delivered as His Discourse to His chosen prophets and through them to all peoples in their languages.

Certainty (ar. *yaqīn*): The real meaning of truth.

Character (ar. *khuluq*): The ensemble of virtues and their opposites as configured in human selfhood.

Charity (ar. *ṣadaqa*): The virtue of giving to another, whereby we bear witness to our responsibility before God and His creation, admitting that everything we have has been received from the Creator.

Clemency (ar. *ḥilm*): A condition of human nature realized through relationship with God the Clement.

Clement (ar. *al-Ḥalīm*): Divine name and term for God as well as for an individual whose character is brought to realization through clemency or relationship with God the Clement.

Conditioned v. Finitude.

Confession v. Witness.

Confidence (ar. *amāna*): God's offer of free will as the condition for establishing the relationship of the Debt (debtor-Creditor) on the basis of confidence or mutual faith.

Conscious (ar. *al-Khabīr*): Divine name and term for one who realizes his character through relationship with God.

Corruption (ar. *fasād*): Whatever is contrary to moral and spiritual wholeness and rectitude.

Covenant (ar. *'ahd*): The compact between God and humankind as His creatures.

Coverer (ar. *kāfir*): A human being whose character is determined by his or her relationship to phenomena that cover or conceal God as the original, authentic, and ultimate Creditor, to whom we owe everything that forms part of our reality.

Covering (ar. *kufr*): The condition of the self determined by its relationship to phenomena denying the nature of divine sign.

Creation (ar. *khalq*): God's expression of His love; the complementary of the Real.

Creator (ar. *al-Khāliq*): Divine name and term for God as well as for an individual whose character is brought to realization through the divine creation and the guidance of the Creator and Guide.

Cube (ar. *Ka'ba*): The simplest form of building and so a sign of our ability to realize His original and authentic potential through doctrine and ritual.

Darkness (ar. *ẓulm*): Covering of the light or the condition of deficient self-realization; lack of form, injustice.

Day of Debt v. Day of Resurrection.

Day of Reckoning v. Day of Resurrection.

Day of Resurrection (ar. *yawm al-qiyāma*): The resurrection of all human beings before the Day of Debt (ar. *yawm al-dīn*) and Day of Reckoning (ar. *yawm al-ḥisāb*); the raising of the bodies of the dead will follow on the annihilation of all creation (ar. *al-fanā' al-muṭlaq*).

Debt, Obligation, or Bondage (ar. *dīn*): The relationship between God as the Creator who indebts and human being as indebted creature under an obligation or bond.

Debtor: One who because of the relationship of confidence or mutual good faith recognizes the debt to God.

Decree (ar. *qadā'*): God's decree for all His creation.

Dignity v. Righteousness.

Disciple (ar. *murīd*): One with the will to avail of the signs and Tradition to connect with the source of Revelation and so with God as He Who Reveals.

dunyā ar. v. World.

Earth (ar. *'arḍ*): Lowest level of the sensible world, which comprises the earth, the heavens, and everything between. Earth corresponds to body in human being, as the little world or microcosm.

Essence (ar. *dhāt*): The entity itself, as opposed to its attributes.

Explanation (ar. *ta'wīl*): Explanation of the meaning of words, particularly of God's message.

Exterior (ar. *ẓāhir*) v. Interior.

Faith (ar. *īmān*): The relationship of human being as faithful with God as the Faithful; it always includes knowledge and love.

Faithful (ar. *al-Mu'min*): Divine name and term for God or for an individual whose character is realized through faith as relationship with God the Faithful.

Fasting (ar. *ṣawm*): Our obligation to refrain from food, drink, and pleasures of the flesh during the month of Ramadan, so as "to taste" God's independence from mere existence.

Fear (ar. *khawf*): A feeling stimulated by danger, horror, or awe for some person or thing which acts or will act contrary to the will of the person confronted by it/him.

Finitude: The mode of being of all created things, including humanity, which is conditioned or determinate existence limited in time, place, possibility, and knowledge. It is contrasted to both the unconditioned Absolute or Infinite, as one (all-encompassing) pole of existence, and the void, as the other nonexistent pole. Human being is necessarily finite but tends toward the void in vice, deficiency, and hopelessness or toward the Absolute in self-realization in virtue and perfectibility.

Following (ar. *mutāba'a*): Taking the prophet the Praised as one's guide on the way to God.

Forgiving (ar. *al-Ghaffār*): Divine name and term for God or an individual whose character is realized through forgiveness as relationship with the Forgiving God.

Friend (ar. *Walī*): Divine name and term for God or an individual whose character is realized through friendship as relationship with God the Friend.

Friendship: The relationship of two individuals through God the Friend.

Garden v. Paradise.

Gatherer, Assembler (ar. *al-Jāmi'*): Divine name and term for one who has realized his character through gathering or bringing together the real in and through relationship with God the Gatherer. By gathering, God brings together the diversity of His creation into His Unity. It is at the same time the continuous act of His creation.

Gentle (ar. *al-Laṭīf*): Divine name or term for God or an individual whose character is realized through relationship to Gentle God.

Gentleness (ar. *luṭf*): The relationship of human beings to Gentle God.

Guidance (1) (ar. *hidāya*): Relationship of human being as guided and God as the Guide; a divine attribute incarnated in the prophets and messengers; the contrary is deception, incarnated in Iblis and his followers.

Guidance (2) (ar. *hudā*): The World, Man, and the Book, through which God guides people toward Himself as the final end of their creaturehood.

Guide (ar. *al-Hādī*): Divine name and term for God or an individual whose character is realized through guidance as relationship with the Guiding God.

hadith v. Tradition.

hajj v. Pilgrimage.

Happiness (ar. *sa'āda*): Bliss, particularly that of Paradise; the opposite of the misery and wretchedness of Hell.

Heart (ar. *qalb*): The innermost kernel of the human self and the locus of our most immediate link with Intellect, first creature and bearer of the meaning and purpose of everything that is in both the invisible and visible worlds; the kernel of consciousness and site of encounter with God.

Heavens, the (ar. *samā'*): The visible upper layer of the created world that faces the earth: The heavens, the earth, and everything in between are signs of the spirit, the body, and the soul.

Hell (ar. *jahannam*): Our nadir or the depth of our fall, which we are led to through forgetfulness of God manifested through pride and meanness as obstacles to humility and generosity; maximum distance from God as the Real.

Holiness (ar. *quds*): The relationship of anything with God the Holy.

Holy (ar. *al-Quddūs*): Divine name and term for God or an individual whose character is realized through relationship with God as Holy.

Honesty (ar. *ikhlās, ṣidq*): Behavior in accordance with God, without consideration of created things, except to the degree God so commands, the opposite of hypocrisy.

Hour (ar. *Sā'a*): The presence of the Real and its final judgment on all phenomena in this and the future world.

House (ar. *bayt*): The place in and through which human beings realizes their original and authentic perfection; its six sides symbolize that all things have both an interior and an exterior and that Peace is the heart of them all.

Human being (ar. *insān*): The Being which gathers in itself all names.

Human Nature (ar. *fiṭra*): Original and authentic human witness to God the Creator.

Humility (ar. *tawāḍu'*): Modesty, acceptance of one's own deficiencies, and acceptance that as a human being one necessarily falls short of what one should or could be, in particular with regard to realization in the self of the divine names. Relationship to the other, based on humility, should always be mediated by consciousness of one's own deficiency in relation to God and the divine names and the essential equality of the other in this regard. A virtue whereby human character is revealed as the image of the divine names and manifestation of the Real.

Hypocrisy (ar. *nifāq*): The unrealized human relationship toward things in the world and in the self and inability to bear witness to the Real who reveals them in eternity.

Hypocrite (ar. *munāfiq*): A human being of unrealized or unformed character, who pretends to be what he is not and so betrays what he is in his relationship to God and to that which veils Him in human consciousness.

Iblis: Personal name of Satan.

Identity: Essentially a Christian term that means the ideal that a human being be the same as Jesus Christ. In the Muslim tradition, identity is the same as unity and means the overcoming of all difference, return to God, or realization that there is no god but God. Due to the fact that everything in existence reveals God, identity is recalled by whatever is in the world or self and so has dignity. Personal identity or identification with one of the various ethnic or religious traditions is, therefore, identification with the eternal values or divine names as refracted through that tradition, but following the Praised (Muhammad) as the principle of everything that is created and as the best example.

Idol (ar. *sharīk*): Anything in existence that is associated or equated with God and to which His attributes are attributed.

Image (ar. *ṣūra*): An image that contains many divine signs in highly condensed form whether in the form of things from the external world (the heavens, the earth, or what lies between), the human self, or the whole or some part of the Book.

Imaginal: Of or belonging to the faculty of the constitutive imagination, whereby our experience of the phenomenal world is given form by recollection of the divine images, which gather material existence into forms that reveal intellectual reality. It thus tends toward the Absolute, and its link to reality distinguishes it strongly from the merely imaginary or free phantasy, which tends toward the void.

iman ar. v. Faith.

Incomparability (ar. *tanzīh*): Opposite of similarity (ar. *tashbīh*).

Injustice (ar. *ẓulm*): Overstepping the boundaries of just action; veiling of the truth, doing wrong to another or oneself.

Inscription: Human being is an inscription of the divine word, insofar as the Word of the Covenant is inscribed within us as potential. This is the innermost meaning of human nature. See also *transcription*.

Intellect (ar. *'aql*): The first creation of God and the indivisible principle of everything that is in the diversity of existence.

Interior (ar. *bāṭin*): Opposite to the exterior (ar. *ẓāhir*); the territory of the spirit, of meaning, and of the heart, as opposed to the body and form.

Interpretation (ar. *tafsīr*): Explication of the meaning of the Recitation; often in contrast to mere explanation (ar. *ta'wīl*); an attempt to descend into or ascend above the text.

Inviolable v. Sacred.

Ishmael (ar. *Ismā'īl*): Abraham's firstborn, prophet of God, participant in the restoration of the Ka'ba and direct ancestor of the Prophet Muhammad.

islam ar. v. Peace.

ism ar. v. Name.

Israel (ar. *Isrā'īl*): Later name of the prophet Jacob, son of the prophet Isaac, and grandson of the prophet Abraham. His descendants are called after him the Sons of Israel.

jahannam ar. v. Hell.

jAnnah ar. v. Paradise.

Jerusalem: The "City of Peace" or earthly sign of the return of human self-hood from the void to Unity and Peace; one of the two holy cities whose focal points are respectively the Sacred or Inviolable Mosque and the Furthest Mosque, which signify the full range of human possibility through our descent from the most beautiful righteousness to the void and our return and redemption.

Jesus (ar. *Īsā*): The Word of God, Prophet of God, son of Mary, the Anointed, to whom God revealed the Good News.

Jews (ar. *yahūd*): A people whose history was shaped by a covenant with God and around the *Torah*, and other books, which together make up God's discourse through his prophets in the language of that people.

Justice (1) (ar. *al-'Adl*): Divine name or term for God or for one whose character is realized in relation to the Just God.

Justice (2) (ar. *'adl, qisṭ*): Just action in accordance with God's will; telling and declaring the truth.

Justness or right (ar. *ḥaqq*): Our duty to recognize our debt to God and the things of His creation, as created and directed by the Creator. By recognizing the justness of everything we confess our debt to God and so our right to redemption.

Ka'ba: A cubic edifice at the heart of the Mecca valley, which, according to tradition, is associated with Adam's arrival on the Earth and, according to revelation, with the prophets Abraham and Ishmael, who restored it and the forgotten right of pilgrimage or hajj; the authentic significance of the Ka'ba was renewed by the Revelation of the Messenger Muhammad and through his example of being-at-peace with God's commandments.

kāfir ar. v. Coverer.

Knowledge (ar. *'ilm, ma'rifa*): The relationship between the knower and the object of his knowing. God has absolute knowledge, which is revealed in his creation. Therefore, the knowledge of any given creature involves ascension toward God as the source and form of all knowledge, embracing everything with His knowledge. Human knowledge, therefore, always falls short and is destructive when mistakenly taken as independent and self-sufficient, with its source outside the Self. Human being has only two sources of knowledge: that which is innate and partakes of Intellect and that which is taken over from others or the world.

Language or tongue (ar. *lisān*): Speech or discourse whereby individual thoughts may be given meaningful utterance using the sounds, words, and phrases that make up the means of communication of a given linguistic community.

Law (Sharia) (ar. *sharī'a*): This concept relates broadly to the debt or obligation of being-at-peace; more narrowly, it denotes the legal teaching of the debt of being-at-peace, in contrast to the way and reality as inner content; the way to human happiness.

Life (ar. *ḥayāt*): The relationship of human being and every other living thing with the Living God.

Light (ar. *nūr*): Divine name and term for God or for an individual whose character is realized through relationship with God as Light.

Living (ar. *al-Ḥayy*): Divine name and term for God or for one whose character is realized through relationship with the Living God.

Lord (ar. *Rabb*): As Lord of all the worlds (*Rabb al-'ālamīn*), God is the Provider, Sustainer, and so forth of all that exists.

Love (ar. *maḥabba, wudd*): Relationship of human being as loving/beloved and God as Loving/Beloved.

Loving (ar. *al-Wadūd*): Divine name and term for God and for one whose character is realized through love for the Loving God.

Macrocosm (ar. *al-'ālam al-kabīr*): The world as a whole, in contrast to the microcosm or lesser world (ar. al-*'ālam al-ṣagh īr*), which is human being. The microcosm is an analogy or epitome of the macrocosm.

Magians (ar. *al-majūs*): The original name for the priesthood and followers of the ancient Iranian religion who are, according to the Recitation, a people of the Book.

Mecca (ar. *Makka*): The City in the Sacred Valley, where the prophet Abraham and his son Ishmael restored the Ka'ba and the pilgrimage as a sign of our ritual return to God from the state of "extreme humility," into which humanity had fallen after violating the prohibition of paradise.

Mercy (ar. *raḥmah*): The relationship of human being and All-merciful God.

Messenger (ar. *rasūl*): A messenger entrusted by God with His message for communication to people in their own language and who is the best example of its acceptance.

Messiah (ar. *al-masīḥ*): v. Anointed.

Microcosm v. Macrocosm.

Moses (ar. *Mūsā*): Divine prophet through whom God revealed the *Torah* to men.

Mosque (ar. *masjid*): A place of prostration, which may be anywhere on earth and may be, but is not necessarily, purpose-built—in which human being expresses utter humility before God; existence and everything in it, in expression of complete submission to God.

Mount (ar. *ṭūr*): A sign of our potential to ascend from the Valley or the condition reached because of the fall from perfection, particularly the Mount of the Furthest Mosque.

Muhammad v. The Praised.

muslim ar. v.: Person-of-peace.

nabiyy ar. v. Prophet

nafs ar. v. Soul and self

Name (ar. *ism*): A guarantee that a phenomenon exists or can exist in human imagination and so in speech.

Nature (ar. *ṭabī'a*): The lower world, accessible to the senses; often contrasted to spirit or intellect. The term *nature* also translates the Arabic *ṭab'*, which signifies individual disposition or the condition of a given individual.

Necessity (ar. *wujūb*): Signifies the impossibility that God is not, given that all of existence depends on Him; necessity is the opposite of impossibility (ar. *mumtani'*), which is both the impossible, such as anything other than God, and the (merely) possible (ar. *mumkin*) or permitted (ar. *jā'iz*), which is everything other than God.

Opener (ar. *al-Fattāḥ*): Divine name or term for God and one whose character is realized through relationship with God as Opener.

Opening (1) (ar. *futūḥ, fatḥ*): Discovery, revelation, or inspiration by direct consciousness of God.

Opening (2) (ar. *al-Fātiḥa*): The first image (ar. *sura*) of the Recitation or the "seven signs (ar. *āyat*) that repeat."

Other (ar. *ghayr*): Everything that is not God; given that God is present to human being wherever he is in everything, the position of the others is unclear.

Other World (ar. *ākhira*): A higher-level world than this one, which accordingly is its sign or visible aspect.

Paradise (ar. *jannat*): The highest condition of humanity in the sensible world, wherein human beings realize or discover their character in relationship with God, as Peace, Faith, and Beauty.

Passion (ar. *hawā*): A condition of the human self in which the spirit-soul-body order is disturbed and subject to changing relations between higher and lower; whims of the soul, or an inner wind that blows the soul to and fro; opposed to intellect, it is the worst of sins, as subjection to the passions means having other gods than God.

Patience (ar. *ṣabr*): The relationship between human beings as patients and God as the Patient.

Patient (ar. *al-Ṣabūr*): A divine name manifest in human nature as self-realization or discovery.

Peace (ar. *al-Salām*): God or one of His most beautiful names.

People of the Book (ar. *ahl al-kitāb*): A people who has during the course of its history received a Revelation from God through one of His prophets.

Perfectibility (ar. *kamāl*): Completion, self-realization; attaining the fullness of the human condition; the process of perfecting certain human qualities; every station on the way to God.

Person-of-peace (ar. *muslim*): A human being who has established an active relationship with God and His signs through being-at-peace, after discovering and realizing God as Peace in his or her own character.

Pilgrimage (ar. *ḥajj*): Obligatory ritual visit to the holy site around the House at Mecca.

Potential: Our original and authentic condition, insofar as we are created with the potential to realize in ourselves the divine names, a potential we fall short of during life, which covering denies and the importance of which is recognized by turning at the House (Ka'ba) from the void toward the Principle and embarking on the upright path. The muslim strives to fulfill his or her potential for self-realization in accordance with the divine names by following the upright path.

Poverty (ar. *faqr*): Our original and authentic condition given that we cannot really possess anything that is not a debt owed to the Creator.

Praised (ar. *al-Ḥamīd*): Divine name and term for God and for one whose character has been realized in relationship with God as Praiser and Praised.

Praised (ar. *Muḥammad*): The last prophet of God, through whom the Recitation was revealed to humanity as the means of our self realization; his name, the Praised, signifies the realization of his character in relationship to God as the All-praised. That which the Praised received thus is manifest in his relationship to God and the World as the nature of the Praised.

Prayer (ar. *ṣalāt*): Individual or collective obligatory ritual address of God, the elements of which were given by God in His Revelation and through the Prophet, the Praised, the best example.

Principle: The first and the source of all that is manifest or created; the Principle as uncreated and uncreatable appears in the manifest and created. The Principle is manifest through different ontological levels. As One, God is the Principle and His creation reveals Him as such.

Prophet (ar. *nabiyy*): A human being or angel/*malak* to whom God has declared His news so that it may be passed on to people.

Prostration (ar. *sajda*): Ritual expression of our extreme humility before God, whereby our contact with the surface of the earth at seven points— forehead, both palms, both knees, and both feet—represents ascent to the seventh heaven or the sublime approach to Peace; by voluntary prostration, along with all of existence, we express God's will through our own or through its annihilation.

Providence (ar. *qadr*): God's comprehension of everything in His knowledge and allocation of clear purpose to existence and everything in it.

Purificatory Alms (ar. *zakāt*): Obligatory expenditure of personal income through which *muslims* cleanse themselves and their property.

Qur'an ar. v. Recitation.

Ramadan (ar.): The ninth month of the lunar year, during which fasting is obligatory.

Real (ar. *al-Ḥaqq*): A name of God or of a human being who has realized or discovered his or her nature through relationship with God as the Real; the name may mean Truth, Justice, Righteousness, and Dignity.

Reality (ar. *ḥaqīqa*): The relationship of human being to God as the Real. Generally, the essence of a phenomenon, the phenomenon-in-itself or as it is known to God.

Realization (ar. *taḥqīq*): The relationship of human being to God as the Real. The Arabic word *muḥaqqiq* refers to one who has attained (self-) realization, which means personal knowledge of the Real within his or her own being. This means seeing things as they really are and acting in accordance with that, which is the condition of the prophets and the good. Self-realization is shaping the self in accordance with the divine names. For us as human beings, being aware means seeing the potential for change in the self for better and for worse; for the worse entails annihilation, for the better means the self embracing everything and resolving the apparent contradictions. Self-realization is reflected in confessing that there is no self but the Self.

Reason (ar. *'aql*): The presence of intellect at the human level, through which human being can compare and take the measure of whatever has sensible existence; our ability to know things in their mutual relations. Taken in isolation from Intellect as an aspect of the Divine, reason appears as instrumental reason, which loses orientation or purpose.

Recitation (ar. *Qur'ān*): The Book sent down by God as His discourse upon the heart of the prophet Muhammad to be communicated to his people in their own language as a warning and as grace.

Redemption (ar. *khalāṣ*): Our right, thanks to and through the execution of good deeds and admission of our debt to God and everything that exists, of our own free will to realize or discover our authentic and original perfection.

Remembrance (ar. *dhikr*): The stimulation of human feelings and consciousness regarding God as the First and Last, the Interior and the Exterior.

Repentance (ar. *tawba*): Turning away from sin toward God.

Revelation (ar. *waḥy*): God's Self-revelation through the created world, through human being, and through His Discourse sent down in the language of men.

Sabaeans (ar. *sābi'ūn*): A people of the Book mentioned in the Recitation.

Sabbath (ar. *sabt*): The seventh day or the return of everything to Peace, which is both the beginning and the end of all things that are in existence.

Sacred (ar. *ḥarām*): That which the Law reveals to be forbidden or illicit; the opposite of what is allowed or licit (ar. *ḥalāl*). That which is inviolable, taboo, sacred.

ṣalat ar. v. prayer.

Satan, the Devil (ar. *shaytān*): This word is used as an alias for Iblis and as a common noun, with a plural, meaning *devil*.

salām v. Peace.

Self (ar. *nafs*): The whole of human existence as comprehended in expression through an *I*. Related to the sense-of-self, personhood, the subject, and subjectivity.

Servant or Bondsman (ar. *'abd*): Any human being or thing in all existence that bears witness to its reality through voluntary or involuntary dependence on the Lord.

Service or Bondage (ar. *'ibāda*): Submission and loyalty; this means executing and following the commandments and rituals arising from being God's servant or bondsman; more loosely, the appropriate human response to God's Reality: namely, witness to unity.

Sign (ar. *āyat*): Everything in existence, which is created with Truth and is therefore Its revelation.

Similarity (ar. *tashbīh*): Expression of the similarity between God and His creatures; opposite to the disclosure of incomparability (ar. *tanzīh*).

Sin (ar. *dhanb, ithm*): Our failure or refusal to live as instructed or required by God, our Creator.

Soul (ar. *nafs*): The transitional area between the body and the spirit; it is split between the soul that tends to evil and the soul that tends to peace.

Speech or Discourse (ar. *kalām*): Any of the possible forms of communicating meaning to a knowing subject; God's speech to His prophets remains a mystery to others except through their own language.

Spirit (ar. *rūḥ*): The highest ontological level in the microcosmic body-soul-spirit order.

Stranger (ar. *'ajamiyy*): A human being who speaks a foreign tongue and so is not intelligible and does not belong to the people of a given language.

Symbol v. Sign.

Tolerance: A relationship between someone who tolerates and someone or something tolerated. Anything in existence has dignity as created with Truth. God asked us to recognize this dignity, according each thing in creation its truth or right. To tolerate means to suffer something that appears wrong, ugly, or unattractive to the tolerating subject. It always involves offense and recognition that the offensiveness of the other and different is a symbol of our own finite nature, while differences are ultimately resolved in the Divine. Tolerance can therefore never involve the reduction of the other to something indifferent and is never indifference.

Torah (ar. *tawrāt*): The Book sent by God to the prophet Moses to be His discourse in human language.

Tradition (1) (ar. *ḥadīth*): The Sayings of the Messenger Muhammad.

Tradition (2): Tradition embraces doctrine, ritual, and virtue, or the knowledge and practice of being human, as established within different human communities through history; each tradition nevertheless transcends history and the world and includes awareness of our transcendent origins, existence, and return to the origin. The sources of tradition are always Intellect and the Word, through which the Divine manifests Himself by means of chosen individuals. Tradition is the school of self-realization.

Transcription: The active discovery and expression of the Word of the Covenant inscribed in us, due to our creaturehood, through our behavior and way of being, in our words, thoughts, and acts, and in particular through doctrine, ritual, and virtue.

Turner (ar. *al-Tawwāb*): Divine name or term for one who realizes his or her character in relationship with God the Turner.

Unity (ar. *tawhīd*): The first expression of the Unseen or mystery, as that which is to be found or which is, independently of anything else through which it is revealed; the testimony throughout existence that there is no god but God. See *identity*.

The Unseen (ar. *ghayb*): That which is beyond every boundary and can never be entirely revealed.

Uprightness, the most beautiful (ar. *aḥsanu taqwīm*): Our original and authentic perfection, the knowledge of all the names, creaturehood in the image of God, unhindered openness toward self-realization through relationship to God, to Whom the most beautiful names belong.

Upright path (ar. *al-ṣirāṭ al-mustaqīm*): A verticality through all levels of Being, from the void to the Absolute, which offers the way of returning to the Self through confession that there is no self but Self and therefore of achieving self-realization in universal or perfect human being.

Valley (ar. *wādī*): Sign of our utmost humiliation after the fall from which we may be raised by purification and ritual to our original and beatific righteousness, particularly the Valley of the Sacred or Inviolable Mosque; the Valley and the Mount together signify the cycle of human descent from beatific righteousness to the depths and the possibility of ascent in the opposite direction.

Void: The conceptual opposite of fullness or the Absolute. It is nonexistence or the nothing toward which human being tends when in error, having strayed from the upright path.

Way (ar. *ṭarīqa, ṭarīq*): The way to God.

Wisdom (ar. *ḥikma*): Our relationship as creatures with God as Wise.

Wise (ar. *al-Ḥakīm*): Divine name and term for God and for one whose character is realized through wisdom in relation to God as Wise.

Witness (ar. *al-Shāhid*): Divine name and term for one who realizes his or her character through witness as a relationship with God as Witness.

Witnessing (ar. *shahāda*): The relationship of a thing or person with God the Witness. The act of witnessing involves both experiencing and confessing the Unity of God, the dependence of existence on God, and that our goal is self-realization after the divine names.

World (ar. *ʿālam*): The totality of all the created, witnessing, and hidden phenomena through which God reveals Himself.

Word (ar. *Kalām*): The principle of divine speech/discourse and the essence of any given linguistic expression.

World, this (ar. *dunyā*): The earth, the heavens, and everything in between that has the attribute of being a sign human being experiences as bearing witness to what lies beyond phenomenal existence.

Worlds: The levels of created existence, from void to the Absolute within which human being takes place and through which it approaches Reality and has mediate experience of Being. They include the noetic, imaginal, and sensible worlds, which correspond to the human faculties of Intellect, Imagination, and Sensible Perception.

Worship (ar. *'ibada*): Submission or devotion; it entails performing and obeying commands and rituals; it is the appropriate human response to the reality of God reflected in the witness of Unity.

ABRAHAMIC DIALOGUES

Donald Moore, S.J., *Martin Buber:*
Prophet of Religious Secularism

James L. Heft, S.M., ed., *Beyond Violence:*
Religious Sources of Social Transformation in Judaism,
Christianity, and Islam

Rusmir Mahmutćehajić, *Learning from Bosnia:*
Approaching Tradition

Rusmir Mahmutćehajić, *The Mosque:*
The Heart of Submission

Alain Marchadour, A.A., and David Neuhaus, S.J.,
The Land, the Bible, and History:
Toward the Land That I Will Show You

James L. Heft, S.M., ed., *Passing on the Faith:*
Transforming Traditions for the Next Generation of Jews,
Christians, and Muslims

Rusmir Mahmutćehajić, *On Love: In the Muslim Tradition*

Phil Huston, *Martin Buber's Journey to Presence*

Philip A. Cunningham, Norbert J. Hofmann, S.D.B., and
Joseph Sievers, eds., *The Catholic Church and the Jewish*
People: Recent Reflections from Rome

Thomas Michel, S.J., ed., *Friends on the Way:*
esuits Encounter Contemporary Judaism

Rusmir Mahmutćehajić, *Across the River: On the Poetry*
of Mak Dizdar. Translated by Saba Risaluddin, with poetry
translations by Francis R. Jones